COURTNEY SHELLEY

# Eat Yo Own Spaghetti

*Reflections on Life, Love, and Reclaiming Your Power*

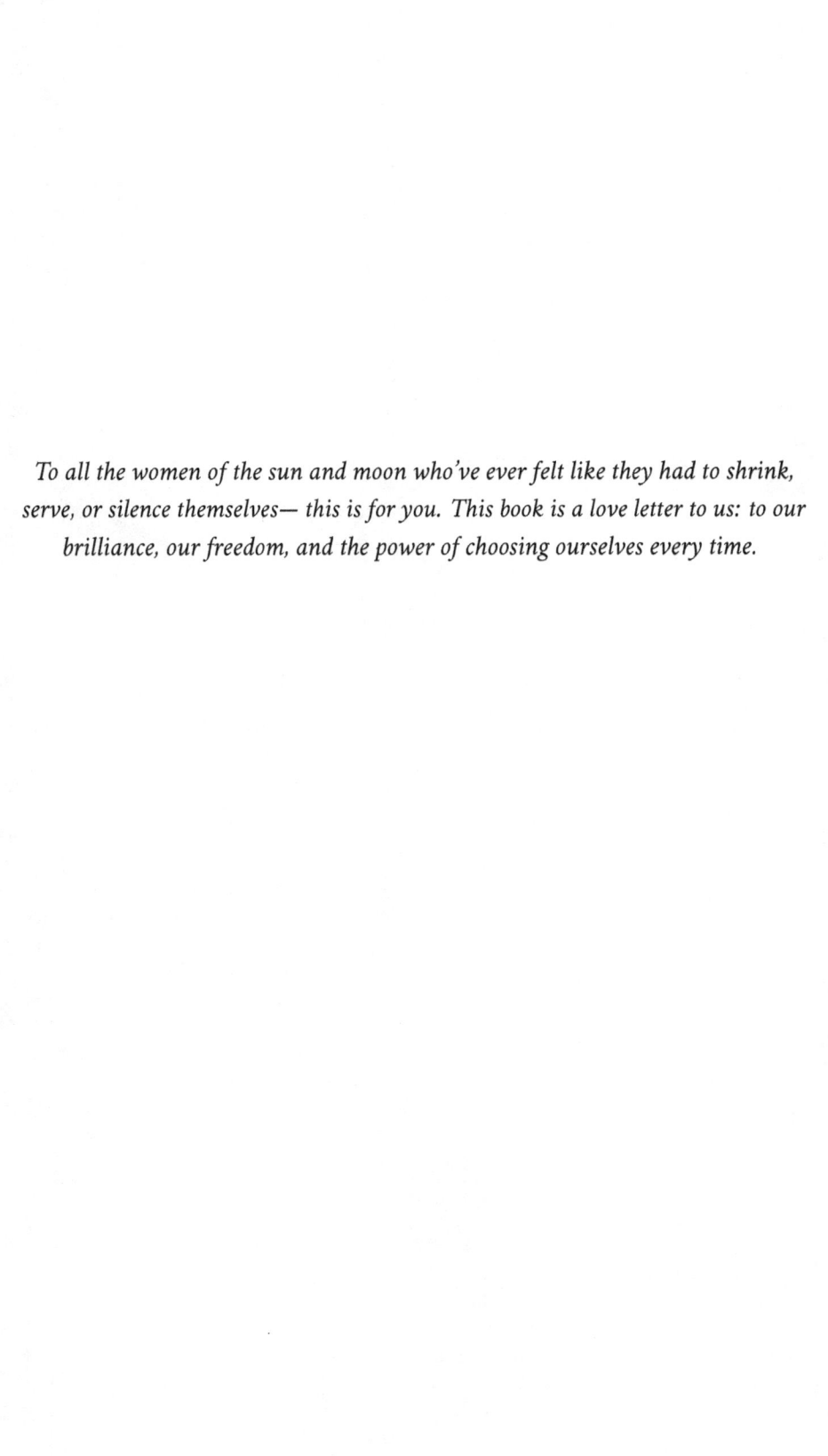

*To all the women of the sun and moon who've ever felt like they had to shrink, serve, or silence themselves— this is for you. This book is a love letter to us: to our brilliance, our freedom, and the power of choosing ourselves every time.*

# Contents

VII   Welcome Home

# Acknowledgments

To my family—thank you for loving me through every version, even when I was unraveling and rebuilding at the same time. Your presence has been my grounding.

To the friends who listened to my voice notes, read my musings, and held space for me when I doubted the sound of my own voice—this book carries your fingerprints. Thank you for seeing me, again and again.

To the Creator—thank you for the whispers, the signs, and the strength to keep going when I had every reason to stop. This was always bigger than me.

And to every version of myself that had to fall apart so I could write this down: I see you, I thank you, and I honor you. You survived. And now, we bloom.

# I

come eat

# Foreword

Some books come in order.
This one doesn't.
It won't hand you a timeline.
It won't walk you from beginning to end like a straight path.
Because that's not how healing moves.

It loops.
It spirals.
It skips steps, then takes you back to the same lesson
until you finally see it clearly.

And then it lets you go.
If you let it.
This is a book made from my memories, my metaphors, my meaning-making—
some hard, some holy, some hilarious.
A collage.
A conjure.
A love letter.
A reclamation.

Some chapters will feel like prayers.
Some like gut punches.
Others might make you laugh at something you swore you'd buried.

Good.
Let it all live here.

Because healing for us—black women—
has never been linear.

We grieve through laughter.
We carry rage in our purses like lip gloss,
pull it out only when we think no one's watching.

There's no right way to read this.
Start at the beginning. Jump around. Come back later.

Just don't rush.

Eat slow.
Feel deep.
Stay with yourself.

And if you brought your grief, your softness, your anger—
good.

Bring all of it. You'll need it.
Welcome to the table

# Eat Yo Own Spaghetti

Everybody knows—you don't eat just anybody's spaghetti.
Especially if you got roots in the South.

It's more than a saying. It's a warning.
A whisper passed down from grandmothers, aunties, barbershops, and
cookouts alike.

Watch what you eat. Watch who you eat from.
The message was always loudest to men—Be careful with that woman. Watch
your plate.

A warning, wrapped in fried fish and folding chairs.
A kind of front-porch folklore passed off as gossip—but always said with a
side-eye, like it came from experience.

The story goes: A woman, desperate to make a man stay, slips a drop of her
own blood into his spaghetti. One bite, and he's bound to her forever.
A love spell. A binding. A tie that won't break.

That's the story we've been told, right?
But maybe the real question was never *what's* in the spaghetti.

Maybe it's: Why would a woman feel she had to bind a man to begin with?
What made staying so urgent? So strategic?

Because once upon a time, a man walking out didn't just break a heart—it could break a home. It could mean a woman with no legal rights. No money. No safety net. No protection. And no power in a world that wasn't built to protect her.

Especially if she was Black.

For us, love has never been just love.
It has been protection. Survival. Security.

When your world is built to take from you—your land, your lineage, your language—the only power you have is what you refuse to let go of.

That's where the magic—our magic—came in.
Because when the world gave us nothing, we created rituals to keep what we loved.
Spells. Intentions. Bindings.

Not always to trap someone.
But to keep from losing everything.

Spaghetti Magic.
A binding.
A way to hold someone close when the world made leaving easy.

But binding is sticky. It's not just spells—it's intention. Presence. Connection.

We've all done it—held onto something too long: a person, a dream, an identity—hoping it would fit, unaware we were stuck.
Binding isn't just making someone stay—it's what you carry when they do.
Expectations. Unfinished energy. Lingering things, long after release.

No, I've never bound a man.
But I've been bound:
To dreams I'd outgrown.
Identities no longer mine.
Versions of success I never chose.

And if you've felt tied, you know what I mean.
Binding itself ain't the problem—it's who and what we choose.

Ancestors bound themselves to love, family, survival—because in a world
built to strip us bare, binding was power.
But not every tie holds safely.
Some keep you stuck.

And before you side-eye Spaghetti Magic, ask yourself this:

- Ever refused to put your purse on the floor because that's how you go
  broke?
- Thrown salt over your shoulder, just in case?
- Knocked on wood? Burned incense? Lit a candle—not just for scent,
  but to shift the air in the room?
- Thrown someone's clothes outside after a breakup—not just out of
  anger, but to clear their energy?
- And don't lie—when grandma dreamt about fish, didn't you immediately
  wonder who was pregnant?

If you said yes?

You're already closer to Spaghetti Magic than you think.
Even when we think we've left those old practices behind, they're still in us.
The rituals might change—but the instinct?
That don't go nowhere.

Because we're still having the same conversations:
Love. Survival. Security.

We don't call it Spaghetti Magic anymore, but the instinct remains—to hold
on, to protect, to make sure we're okay.

Love for us was never just affection.
It was strategy.
It was resistance.
It was survival.

Done right: it's power.
Done wrong: it's ruin—soul, mind, wallet, body.

We've left some rituals behind, but today's relationship debates still echo the
same instinct:
"What do you bring to the table?"
"Who's paying what?"
"Should a woman build with a man or wait for him to be ready?"

These aren't just dating questions.
They're survival questions.
They're about who stands beside you when the world wants you to fail.

Spaghetti Magic got reduced to a punchline:
A desperate woman.
A pot of noodles.
A drop of blood.
A shame.

But the magic was never in the sauce.
It was always in the woman.

Her essence.
Her intention.
Her ability to transform scraps into something sacred.

She wasn't trapping.
She was surviving.

But here's what they never told us—
The most powerful binding isn't to another person.
It's to yourself.
To your purpose.
To your becoming.
To the vision you have for your life—even if nobody else sees it yet.

You don't need to slip anything into anyone else's plate to be chosen.
Choose you.
Bind yourself to you.
Feed yourself first.
That's what it means to eat your own spaghetti.
The truth got twisted.
But now?
It's time to snatch our bowl back.
Make our own meal.
Serve ourselves.
And savor every bite.

Because Spaghetti Magic was never about holding someone down.
It was about refusing to be powerless.
Once you realize that, everything shifts.

Yes, I'm telling this through my lens—my lessons, my grief, my growth.
But this ain't just about me.
It's about you too.

Whether you've given too much, struggled with boundaries, sat in grief, or carried rage that has nowhere to go—you know the feeling.
The bind.
The pull.
The weight.

Just like I had to learn to eat my own spaghetti—so do you.

> *This is a journey of heartbreak and healing.*
> *Of rage and rest.*
> *Of falling apart and coming home to yourself.*
> *Of setting boundaries.*
> *Reclaiming power.*
> *And falling in love—not just with someone else, but with you.*

So let's be clear—this spaghetti ain't about a man.
It's about your voice.
Your boundaries.
Your becoming.

> This ain't no spell book.
> Unless, of course, you're ready to conjure yourself back.

And if you are—go on and get your plate, it's time to eat.

# The Recipe

**Ingredients:**

6 ounces of release

1 deep breath of patience

5 dashes of resilience

2 turns of wisdom

4 clean cuts of boundaries

10 tablespoons of self-worth

11 strokes of clarity

4 splashes of acid

3 heartbeats of love

Roast what no longer serves you—let it char, let it go

   Oven-bake the lessons slow, give them time to rise

   Nourish what feeds your soul, not what leaves you hollow.

   Quick-sear the moments that burned, but left you wiser.

   Undercut the weight of dead things

   Infuse your days with love, thick like butter, rich like truth.

   Simmer in your own magic—low heat, no rush, let it build.

   Emulsify the past—blend pain and power into something smooth.

   Vinegar-cure the wounds—let them sting, then let them strengthen.

   Extract the wisdom, separate the lesson from the loss.

   Aromatize your presence—walk in, let them feel you before you speak.

   Layer every love, every loss, every lesson—this is the recipe.

**Yields:** A dish too bold to be bitter, too rich to be wasted, and too well-seasoned to be anything but unforgettable.

**Chef's Note:** And listen, it ain't spaghetti unless you add a little sugar—non-negotiable. Because life, just like tomatoes, can be acidic as hell sometimes. That little sugar? It balances the bite, softens the edges, makes it something worth savoring. That's the alchemy our grandmothers' grandmothers mastered long before we got here. They knew how to sweeten their stories, no matter what got thrown in the pot. So like my mama, sprinkling a pinch of sugar over her spaghetti—don't forget to add yours. Life is yours to season.

# Atlanta Wing Order

In Atlanta, your wing order might as well be your love language.
Lemon pepper wet? You want flavor and attention.
Extra crispy? You don't play about texture or treatment.
Peach drink on the side? You like a little sweetness to balance the heat.

Ordering wings here isn't just about taste—it's a statement.
A blueprint.
A low-key biography in takeout form.

The first time I ordered from an American Deli in Atlanta, I was a freshman at Georgia State—away from home, broke, and still figuring out what I wanted... in life and in wings.

The girl in front of me? A certified ATL-ien. Box braids in a ponytail, walked like she owned the sidewalk.

Her voice? Crisp. No hesitation. Every syllable served a purpose.

She stepped up before the cashier could even greet her:
*"Let me get a 10-piece hot lemon pepper sprinkles, extra wet, extra crispy, peach drink, and make sure my fries fresh 'cause they wasn't last time."*

It wasn't just the flavor combo that hit. It was the confidence.
The clarity.

The way she said what she wanted without flinching.

That's the thing: life works the same way.
The more specific you are about what you want, the more likely you are to get it. Whether it's relationships, careers, or goals—clarity is power.

Too many of us live like we're placing a vague order—hoping people or circumstances will guess our needs.

But if you don't know what you want, how can anyone—or anything—give it to you?

Getting there means looking within.
Reflecting on what lights you up and what drains you.
Learning from what worked—and what didn't.

It's trial, error, and attention.

The girl at the counter? She didn't wake up knowing her perfect wing combo.
She earned it—bite by bite, mistake by mistake.

Life is no different.

I used to settle for the spiciness of a nonchalant guy—the kind who keeps you guessing.

But as I grew, I realized I wanted more: a hot honey energy—someone kind, attentive, with just enough kick to keep it interesting.

But even when I figured that out, I hit a new wall: fear of demanding it.

We've all been there.

You get your fries, but they're cold.
You don't say anything.
Cause you don't wanna be "that person."
You convince yourself it's fine.

But really—who are you cheating?
By the time I finally found my flavor, I had a long history of accepting whatever was handed to me.
In love. In work. In life.

When you're used to settling, demanding more feels like conflict.

But it's really just clarity.

You have a choice:
Accept what's handed to you, or ask for what you deserve.

And if they can't give it to you?
You find somewhere else that can.

Knowing what you want is one thing. But having the boldness to ask for it?
That's the real shift.

You can't mumble your order and expect excellence.
You have to say it with your chest—
    "Make sure those wings are extra crispy, because last time they weren't, and I'm not doing that again."

That's power.

That's self-trust.
Life demands the same.
No one's handing you the perfect relationship, career, or peace.

You have to claim it.

That means saying:
"This is what I want. This is how I want it. And I'm not settling for less."

The more you practice asking for what you want, the more natural it becomes—and the more often you'll get it.

So here's the question:

**What's your order?**

Are you settling for whatever life hands you, or are you stepping up to the counter, clear and confident in what you deserve?

Because life's too short for soggy wings and half-baked dreams.

Know what you want.
Demand it.
And if they get it wrong—
**Send. It. Back.**

**Check Your Order**

- What's your "10-piece, extra wet, extra crispy" in life—your personal flavor combo that feels like you?
- Where have you been settling for cold fries and convincing yourself it's

enough?

- When was the last time you said your order with your whole chest?
- What's one thing—relationship, expectation, opportunity—you're finally ready to send back?

# Caught Up In The Rapture

We almost never met.

I wasn't even supposed to work that night—picked up the shift last minute.
An hour in, they asked if I wanted to take my first party. I almost said no.

But when they offered all the tips if I ran it solo, something in me leaned
forward.

I gripped my notepad like a lifeline.

And then—I saw him.

Laughing mid-joke, head tilted back, loud enough to turn heads.

He didn't just sit at the table—he commanded it.
He moved like he expected the world to catch up.
Like life bent itself around him.

Meanwhile, I was just trying not to drop the tray.

He watched me—curious, open, like he already had a question forming.
That look made me feel seen in a way I hadn't realized I was waiting for.

Not to be corny—but it felt electric.

Like recognition without reason. A pull. A pause.

Something flickered back to life.

It was the kind of moment I'd only read about—
the kind of love I used to sneak from my mama's stash.

Bent paperback covers with women in satin and men behind them,
hands firm on their hips like both a promise and a possession.

Those books made love feel like magic.
And suddenly, I was inside one.

Before I even left the parking lot that night, he texted me.

That one message unraveled into a thread—music, food, memories, dreams.

Every time it seemed like the conversation would end, it spun into something
new.

He started showing up at my job.
In my section. In the parking lot.

Waiting—for a hug, a kiss, or nothing but a look.
No reason. Just presence.

And that alone made me feel exhilarated—
like I had found someone who thought I was worth showing up for.

Our first date was simple.

Soda drinks. A walk in the park.
Then the skate park, where he laced up and glided like he was born to fly.

I stood there, stunned by how free he looked.

I didn't know how to name the ache that rose watching him.
It was part awe, part longing.

I wanted to move like that.
Laugh like that.
Exist like that.

That summer, I fell—hard.

We filled our days with stolen moments.
Parking lot kisses. Random errands.
Nights that stretched like warm vinyl.

He introduced me to his world, to the people who knew him best.
And I watched, spellbound by how effortlessly he moved through it.

I was always in my head—analyzing, holding back.
He lived in the moment, untethered.

With him, I had to step out of observation mode and become an active
participant.
The love we were curating required my presence—
not just my witnessing.

I couldn't just read the story anymore.
I had to be in it.

It was the kind of love that made me scribble poems on server notepads.

Lines about passion burning up the ordinary.
Love that made you speed through yellow lights instead of coasting through

greens.
Love I thought only lived in fiction—until him.

He wasn't perfect.

Messy. Loud. Chatty.

The most beautiful liar I'd ever met.

And maybe, deep down, I knew that.
But I stayed—not because I didn't see the signs,
but because of how he made me feel.

Alive. Seen. Unfiltered.

He reminded me of someone I used to be.

As a child, I was bold. Opinionated. Loud.
Moved through the world without hesitation—
before I learned to shrink for safety, for belonging, for control.

With him, I wasn't on the sidelines.
I was in it.
Feeling everything.

And I convinced myself that was enough.

That summer, we made a list of everything we wanted to experience together.
For a moment, it felt like time would stretch forever.
Like we'd keep adding to that list until the paper ran out.

But I wasn't just falling in love with him.
I was falling in love with the version of me that came alive in his presence.

I wasn't clinging to a man.
I was clinging to the feeling of being seen.

Seen in the way he studied me.
Noticed things I was still learning myself.
Remembered stories I didn't know I'd shared.

Seen when his eyes scanned the room and found mine.
Seen when no one else had been looking.

Our days were full of heat and sunshine,
and our nights—drenched in possibility.

A brewing Category 5 hurricane of first love.
Soft and wild. Sweaty and new.

But even the sweetest summers cast shadows.

And whether you see it coming or not—
**summer always ends.**

# Applebees Circa 2014

when it's ten years down
the line I promise
you I'll
still get nervous about
what I'm going to

The kind of love that
puts butterflies in my
stomach long after
your hair turns gray
and our bones began to
hurt.

I want the kind of love
where I keep a notebook
nearby so I can write down
all the things I want to
say to you but when I
get around I get lost in your
eyes

The

APPLEBEES CIRCA 2014

I want love...
Not the stuff that people
call love nowadays
not that warmed up
tolerance people build
lives off of but
the flames we all strive
for.

The stuff that melts you
just thinking about someone
made just for you.

Not a love that you can live
for but one that you'll die
for.
a love that makes you
speed through yellow lights
instead of coasting through
greens
I know I'm asking for a lot
but that's all I want.
Not comfortability but
passion.
The kind that wakes you in
from the inside out
The kind of love where
we never stop trying.

APPLEBEES CIRCA 2014

# //Notes App- 2018: The List

**good things:**
- Makes me laugh
- Caring and dependable (especially with other people)
- Gives good advice sometimes
- Kisses me like I'm the only woman in the world
- Gives me butterflies[1]
- Remembers little things I say and surprises me with them
- Protective of me
- Sex feels spiritual when we're connected..when its good its *goooooodd*
- Has a big ego… as Beyoncé would say
- Said my love feels like heaven[2]

**bad things:**
- Gets angry easily
- Ignores me[3]
- Has too many female "friends"[4]
- Doesn't pay me back quickly[5]
- Is messy
- Can be a know-it-all
- Lazy sex
- Makes me feel crazy
- Tried to push me in front of a moving car[6]
- Does not show me affection
- Lies to me

**footnotes:**

[1] *child. anywaysss.*

[2] *yeah he would know. Lucifer knew what heaven looked like too. lol. let me stop.*

[3] *cause he know he saw me calling him.*

[4]*yeah. I was right. He was fucking them bitches.*

[5] *cause why I gotta remind you for my money back?*

[6] *okay, so here's what happened—we were in the French Quarter, walking (irritated), and I was in front of him. He hit me with one of those impatient "come on" nudges... and a car was literally coming. Like, moving. And y'all know the driving down there in New Orleans is questionable at best. So yeah... a bitch could've died.*

II

crybaby

# Ain't Nobody Died

I was born a crybaby. I was always that kid who didn't hold back when something hurt me or when something didn't feel right. I can trace it back to one of the first lessons I ever learned about feeling things—and hiding them.

## The First Betrayal

In kindergarten, I had a best friend. We were inseparable—or so I thought. One day during color time, most kids grabbed white construction paper, but I was drawn to the black. Something about it felt different, like it could bring my idea to life. I told her my plan: I wanted to draw a moon and ocean scene. I was so proud of it. But when I came back to grab the black paper—it was gone.

She took it. And not just the paper—she took my idea too.

I stood there, stunned. Betrayed.

When I snapped at her, my teacher said I was behaving inappropriately.

When I asked how to spell "hate," because that's how deeply I felt it, she refused—and moved my clip to red.

I asked to go to the restroom. I needed somewhere to go.
Somewhere to release it.
In that stall, I screamed. I cried.
Because crying made me feel better.
But I got in trouble for the scream too.
As if releasing the pain was worse than the betrayal itself.

## Learning to Hide

As a little girl, my parents tried to understand my big feelings. But as I got
older, the space for my emotions got smaller. If I cried too long, it became:
   **"Why are you doing all that crying? Ain't nobody died."**
That message planted itself deep. I still cried—but in secret.
I'd wait until I was alone, put on the saddest music I could find—Aaliyah's
*Never No More*, or Tank's *Cry*—crawl under the covers, and let the tears fall.
Afterward, I always felt clearer. Like something had lifted off my chest.
But I learned to treat that softness like a secret.
Because if other people couldn't hold it, maybe I shouldn't either.

## Becoming the Mask

What happens when your superpower—your ability to feel deeply—is
mistaken for weakness?
You start to mute yourself.
You blunt your edges.
You become strategic about when and where your emotions are safe.
I started calculating my feelings instead of feeling them.
And that numbness? It sneaks in quiet.
You move through life checking boxes—career, milestones, friendships—but

something still feels... off.
And when I tried to share that ache with others, they'd say:
"Girl, you're good. Don't worry about that."
But I did worry. I was performing stability while quietly unraveling.

## The Skinned-Knee Kind of Grief

When my long-term relationship ended—the one I spent my 20's in—I didn't
fall apart. I just... kept moving. Went to work. Answered calls. Cleaned the
house. But inside? I was skinned-knee raw. The adrenaline had worn off,
and now the sting was setting in. It took me a while to realize what I was
feeling wasn't just heartbreak—it was grief.

## Invisible Grief

We talk about grief like it only shows up when someone dies.
But grief is layered.
It's the job you thought would change your life but didn't.
The version of you that didn't survive a season.
The expectations that never made it to reality. Grief is the playlist from a
better year. The T-shirt you never threw away. The dinner table with one
chair still pulled out. It's the life that never arrived. There's no funeral for
the life you thought you'd have. No eulogy for the girl you used to be.
But the grief is real.
Some loves don't just end—they become ghosts.
You carry them.
Not just the love that ended, but the person you were inside of it.

# The Things That Never Came

There's also the grief of the almosts.
I grieved the relationship that never turned into marriage.
The home we never built. The future we dreamed of that never came.
It wasn't just the end of a relationship—it was the mourning of what never got the chance to exist.

# Giving It Language

Eventually, I stopped asking for permission to grieve. I let the sadness sit beside me. I let the tears come without needing a reason. And somewhere in the quiet of that release, I found myself again.
Not the girl who had it all together.
The one who feels. The one who lets it move through her.
Because the only way out—is through. And the only thing you can do to hold space for the invisible grief that quietly haunts you is to cry...**baby.**

# Welcome To My Upside Down

Life doesn't always tap you on the shoulder and ask if you're ready.
Sometimes, it just snatches you.
No warning. No countdown. No way to prepare.

One second, you're moving through life like normal—minding your business, following your routine. And then? Boom. You're somewhere else. Transported into a version of your life that looks the same but doesn't feel the same.

That's exactly what happened to Will in *Stranger Things*. One moment, he was riding his bike home. The next? Snatched into the Upside Down. At first glance, it looked like home. The same streets. The same houses. But something was wrong.

It was darker. Colder. Heavier. The air felt thick. The world was covered in shadows and vines. Everything looked familiar—but nothing felt the same.
And that?
That's what happened to me.

## My Personal Demogorgon

I didn't walk into this place willingly.

One day, my life was steady. Predictable. Then suddenly? Gone. I was snatched.

For me, the Demogorgon wasn't a monster with claws. It was the ending of a relationship I didn't want to give up. I outran it. I softened myself. I bent. I ignored my intuition. I betrayed myself to keep "us" alive.

And for a while, it worked.

But eventually, the Demogorgon caught up. And when it did, it tore through everything. It wasn't just the loss of a person—it was the collapse of the life I'd built around him.

## The Weight, the Silence, and the Unbothered World

The grief didn't arrive all at once.
It settled in like fog, creeping into everything.
Waking up to no messages.
Silent lunch breaks.
His scent fading from the shirt I wore.
Thumb hovering over the share button before remembering there was no one on the other end.

His absence echoed louder than his presence ever did.
And the silence?
It wasn't soft. It was sharp.
It reminded me of how much space he took up—how deeply woven he'd become in the rhythm of my days.

But the world kept spinning.
Your car still needs gas.
The emails still come in.

You still have to smile at people in the grocery store.
Even when your inside world is unrecognizable.

## Becoming Through the In-Between

The Upside Down makes you believe that acceptance is your way out. That if you just let go, something new will appear. Like surrender is a transaction. But that's not how this works. Letting go isn't the finish line. It's the starting point.

There's that viral image of the little girl and the teddy bear. Jesus asks her to give up her tiny one, hiding a bigger one behind his back. The message? *Trust me. I have something better.*

But what if she lets go and… nothing happens?

What if she's just standing there, empty-handed?

That's what the Upside Down feels like.

A pause.
A silence.
A long stretch between the letting go and the becoming.
A test of trust.

If you see this space as punishment, it will feel like one.But if you reframe it as preparation—as a sacred pause—it shifts. The in-between becomes a classroom. Because this space isn't here to hurt you. It's here to shape the version of you that can hold what's next.The you before? She doesn't live here anymore.The you next? She's still under construction. So instead of asking *"When do I get out?"* ask *"Who am I becoming while I'm here?"*

## The Lifeline

In Season 4, Max becomes haunted by her own version of the Upside Down.
She's fighting invisible forces—depression, grief, guilt.
Things she can't name, but that are trying to consume her.
She's not just running from the monster.
She's trying not to disappear.
And just when it seems like she's slipping too far, her friends blast her favorite
song—Kate Bush's *Running Up That Hill*.

The music becomes her tether. Her lifeline.
It reminds her of who she is. Of what's still real.
You need your own version of that.
It might not be music.

Maybe it's a vision of the life you're rebuilding.
A ritual that brings you back to yourself.
A community that holds you accountable.
A whisper of faith in what's not visible yet.
Whatever it is, hold onto it.

Because the in-between will lie to you.
It will try to convince you to give up.
But your lifeline?
That's how you run toward the opening when it finally appears.

## Learn Before You Leave

Max escaped.
Will didn't.
Because just getting out isn't enough.

In the series, Will was rescued physically—but never emotionally. The trauma stayed with him. He couldn't connect to his old life the same way. He carried what happened in the Upside Down.

If you don't process the pain, it follows you.
If you don't learn the lesson, the pattern repeats.
You have to leave emotionally, spiritually, and mentally.
Not just physically.

## Your New Life Requires a New You

You don't get to bring the old version of yourself into your new life.
This next chapter?
It isn't for the one who settled.
Who silenced herself.
Who ignored her knowing.
It's for the one who rose.

## Trust the Process

This space will make you question everything.
It will whisper that nothing is coming.
But the truth?
It's already on the way.
The only question is: Can you trust yourself long enough to let it arrive?

# RIP Ms. John Redcorn

Some parts of you have to die so that other parts can live.
—Shannon L. Alder

*"We are gathered here today to mourn the passing of Ms. John Redcorn."*
*A devoted healer. A woman who poured and poured until she was empty.*
*Today, we lay her to rest.*
*We thank her for her service, but we will not resurrect her.*
*We will not call her back from the grave.*
*May she rest in power. Never to return again.*

## The Thing About John Redcorn

On the surface, John Redcorn—the side character from *King of the Hill*—was easy to laugh at.
The long-haired, shirtless man locked in a drawn-out affair with Nancy, even as she publicly stayed with her clueless husband, Dale.
Everyone watching could see it.
He was always "the other man." Quiet. Consistent. Predictable.
Stuck in a cycle.

From the outside, it looked foolish. Pathetic, even.
But John Redcorn loved Nancy.

And sometimes, love will have you clinging to something that's clearly breaking you—just because you remember what it felt like before it broke.

There's a lyric in SiR's song "John Redcorn" that always gets me:
*"Alone... every night alone... why am I alone when I know that you want me to?"*

It's not just a song about being used—it's about being stuck.
Stuck in the aching space between what someone says they want and what they're capable of giving.
And the sad part is, there's a part of them that loves you too.
But they can't love you—because they won't let themselves.

That's what Ms. John Redcorn did.
She didn't stay because she didn't know better.
She stayed because her heart kept whispering, *Maybe this time.*


## I've Always Loved Love Movies


The dramatic kind—the ones where two people are so deep in it, they'd rather die than be without each other.

*Titanic* was one of the first to get me.
The way Jack looked at Rose made me wonder if I'd ever be loved like that—
So deeply, so completely, that someone would freeze in the Atlantic just to keep me safe.

Even as a girl, I remember watching that final scene with tears in my eyes.
Jack in the water. Rose on the door. Her lips trembling. His hand slipping.
And that moment when she had to let him go—prying his fingers from the wood, whispering *I'll never let go* while doing just that.

It made me wonder:
Would I ever love like that—and be loved like that in return?
And what would it cost me?

Be careful what you wish for.

## The Man I Fell in Love With

When I first met him, he felt free.
Not because life hadn't touched him—it had.
But because he still moved like it hadn't caught up to him yet.

He had the spirit of someone full of promise.
Big dreams he never stopped chasing, even as life tried to shake them loose.

He was chatty, open, full of laughter.
An early riser. A restless creator.
The kind of person who could pick up a wrench and bring a dead car back
to life like it was nothing.

But even in the beginning, there was something underneath the light.
A heaviness.
A quiet sadness that crept in when he thought no one was looking.

Maybe it had always been there.
Maybe life had already pressed down on him—
He just hadn't let himself feel the full weight of it yet.

Then came the first blows.
Leaving college.
Taking a job that never truly challenged him.

Jumping to another. Then another. Searching for more.

With every shift, the routine pulled him down.
The life that once felt full of opportunity began to feel like a trap.

He needed change like he needed air.
No matter how good something was at first, it never stayed that way for long.
What began as a blessing always turned into a cage.

He was curious to do more. Be more.
But no matter where he went, no matter what he tried—
His demons followed him.

And over time, that restless, hungry part of him that once made him shine began to make him unravel.

## The Wounds He Carried

He was the source of comedy in almost every room.
Sharp-witted, always quick with a joke—
The type who could make a whole group laugh without even trying.

His humor wasn't performative; it was instinctive.
He had a gift for flipping even the mundane into something hilarious.
It was one of the things I loved most—how he could lift the weight from the room.

But over time, I realized: it wasn't just light.
It was armor.

He leaned into the brightest parts of himself
while quietly starving out the darkness.

He wouldn't face his shadows.
He didn't talk about them.
He ran.

He ran for years—until they caught up.
It was a cat-and-mouse game:
He'd live in the light, ignoring the pain chasing him, pretending it didn't
exist.

But demons don't vanish when you look away.
They wait.
And when they strike again, they strike harder.

His pain didn't start in adulthood.
It had roots.
He carried quiet, unresolved resentment toward his mother.
Whether justified or not, it shaped him.
He felt like she chose her relationships over her children.
Like she loved in a way that made him feel unseen. Unprotected. Unlovable.

He once told me a story:
When he was little, he joked that she liked bald men—just like a guy she used
to date.
She slapped him.

He told it with a shrug, like it was funny now.
But there was an edge under the laughter.
A rawness he never processed.

And then, there was his father.

46

A man he barely got to know before losing him forever.

They said he drowned saving someone else.
But later, in therapy, questions came up:
Was it really an accident?
Was there more?

Grief blurred into confusion.
He was just a kid, trying to survive the weight of absence.
Trying to make sense of a story no one finished telling.

And while he was still grieving, they enrolled him in therapy—
A well-meaning move that nearly wrecked everything.

He talked to white therapists with the honesty only children have.
He talked about home. About "whoopings."
And before he knew it, that grief almost turned into a CPS investigation.

Almost losing the only parent he had left.

After that, he didn't trust therapy.
Didn't trust vulnerability.
Didn't trust systems that claimed to help.
Didn't trust anyone to hold his truth without taking something from him.

He used to joke about it—
Say he couldn't go to therapy because someone might jump out the bushes
and 302 him.
But under the joke was truth:
He believed honesty about his pain would always come with a cost.

There was one person, though—
One person he believed saw him fully.

His grandmother.
She knew him. Loved him. Poured into him.
She bought him his first car. And it changed everything.

That car wasn't just transportation.
It was purpose.

It unlocked something in him.
It gave his curiosity a place to land.

Because with cars, there was always something to fix.
Always a puzzle to solve.
Unlike life—where some things broke and stayed broken—
A car was something he could figure out.

Even when others couldn't fix it, he could.
And in those moments, he didn't feel broken.
He felt powerful. Capable. Worthy.

She saw that in him.

But she never got to see him finish.
She passed before she could witness the man he was becoming.
And that haunted him.
He carried it—this feeling of being unfinished.
Like he had failed her.
Like no matter how hard he tried, he'd never become the man she believed
he could be.

So he started to believe he never would.
And once that belief took root...
he stopped trying.

## I Knew Him Like a Song

And I noticed. Because I knew him.
Not just his favorite color or how he liked his coffee. I knew him like a
song. Not just the words, but the feeling. Every note, every shift, every slight
variation was noticeable.

I had learned him. Enmeshed our souls so closely together that hiding
was impossible.The armor he wore—humor, lightness, detachment—was
see-through to me.

It could be the smallest thing. A deprecating joke said too casually. One
word spoken just a little off. I'd catch it.

My mind was tuned to him.
And I was an A+ student. I could sense the slightest change in his tone and
know something was off. And as our bond deepened, he didn't even need to
speak. I could see it in his eyes.

When I saw it, I laced up my shoes to come save him.
Every. Single. Time.
At first, when the darkness called, he called too.
He'd text. Call. Let me know the door was open.
And I would come.

No matter how late, no matter how tired—I would crawl into his bed, into
his arms, into the warmth that was us, and hold him.
I would will away his sadness. Project the version of him I saw—bright,
curious, full of light back into him. Like if I held him close enough, that
energy might seep in.Might restore him. Might bring him home to himself.

But no matter how much I poured in,It was never enough to fill the places

where he had abandoned himself.
Over time, the calls slowed.
The distance grew.
The door that was always open started staying closed.
He pulled back.
Deeper into his abyss—of darkness, vices, self-sabotage.
And I?
I kept coming anyway.
Even when he stopped asking.

## The Slide Into Darkness

He started as a social drinker.
Someone who drank for taste, not need.
On our date nights at Tin Lizzy's, we sipped Thai basil margaritas over chips
and queso.

Drinking was an accessory to the joy.
Never the reason for it.
But something shifted.
He didn't need dinner, company, or celebration to drink anymore.

He started drinking alone.
The cocktails were replaced by whiskey—neat.
A chaser on the side, never enough to soften the burn.

At first, I didn't know what to make of it.
Should I confront him?
Would it push him away?

I tried the soft approach.

Asked why. Encouraged slowness. Urged curiosity.
And he told me, drinking silenced his thoughts.
It was the only thing keeping him from drowning.

It started with: *A drink helps me sleep better.*
Then: *A drink quiets my mind.*
Then: *It calms me down.*
Then: *It's the only thing that stops me from spiraling.*

One became two.
Two became a bottle.
A coping mechanism turned crutch.
Two DUIs.
A functional dependence.

But he wasn't just numbing the present.
He was grieving himself.
Grieving the man he used to be.
The one always in motion. Always fixing. Always figuring things out.

Now he couldn't keep commitments.
To his job. His friends. Himself.
Alcohol became the only thing that softened the scream inside him.
But eventually, even that stopped working.

## The Isolation

And when it stopped working, he withdrew.
The people who loved him tried to pull him back.
They called. Checked in. Showed up.
Tried to hold him steady.

But he resisted.
Because by then, he'd built a new world.
One where no one knew him before the light left his eyes.
In that world, there were no expectations.
No mirrors.

Just people with demons of their own.
People who didn't ask him to grow.
People who didn't challenge the numbness.
He didn't have to explain himself.
He didn't have to try.
He could just... exist.
In the dark.
Unbothered. Unaccountable.

He stopped reaching for those of us who knew him best.
Because he didn't want to be seen anymore.
And still, I stayed.
Still believed I could bring him back.

## The Cost of Loving Him

At first, I showed up willingly. So full of belief. So sure my love could save him. And sometimes, it felt like it was working. I'd hold him. Whisper truths into him. Tell him he was still brilliant. Still worthy. Still full of promise.

He'd look at me with those same eyes.
Eyes of a man who adored me.
A man who, at his best, was affectionate, poetic, soft.
The one who said our love felt like heaven.

But almost like clockwork, the shift would come. Cold. Distant. Unreadable. He'd disappear into distractions. Pull away just enough to remind me he could. I knew both versions were real.

I loved one.
I grew to resent the other.
And the back-and-forth?
It wore me down.

## The Schism

Resentment built. Not just because he was struggling but because he was choosing to stay stuck. I'd watch him light the match. Fan the flame. Sit in the fire. And then lock me out.

Still, I beat on the door.
Still, I tried to pull him out.
Because how could I just watch him burn?
And yet— he seemed mad at me for even trying.
Like I was reckless for loving him through it.

When all I wanted to scream was:
*Why do you keep doing this?*
*Why do you keep hurting yourself—knowing your pain spills over into mine?*
He knew.
But he did it anyway.

## The Change in Me

Loving him was a war. Not some short battle, but one of those long, drawn-out wars that stretch across years.

The kind that starts with belief.
The soldiers are sharp. Hopeful.
Their heads held high as they march through the mud, fueled by certainty that they will win.

At first, I was just like them.
But over time, belief became identity.
I didn't just believe in our love—I *lived* in it.
I built a home inside it.
Swore allegiance to it.
Saving him.
Saving *us*.
That was my flag.

I planted it deep in the ground, and I wasn't leaving without it. I was resilient.
Determined. Steadfast in my love and my belief in him.
Because I believed.
Believed I could reach him.
That my love would call him back to himself.
That we would make it.

But the years wore me down. And like those soldiers, I started to change.
The ones who once moved with clarity now dragged their feet. Uniforms tattered. Hope hanging by a thread. I became cynical.

When he opened up, I didn't always meet him with softness.
I listened for cracks.

For contradictions.
For the ways his words didn't match his actions.
I started assuming the worst.

The typing in the background during our calls?
"Oh, you're texting a bitch?"
The nights he wasn't in the mood to talk?
"Oh, I bet you were talking just fine to somebody else."

I hated who I was becoming.
Suspicious. Guarded. Sharp-edged.
I stopped giving him the benefit of the doubt.
Because I had run out of benefit to give.
I checked his phone.
I tracked his patterns.
I read between every line.

Years of confusion and emotional whiplash turned me into someone who
crashed out.
Pop-ups.
Unannounced pull-ups.
Trying to catch in 3D what my spirit already knew.
And he noticed the change in me.
When he came back mushy, loving, sometimes he met the version of me
who couldn't fully trust anymore.
And when that happened?
He pulled back.

Further.
And further.
Until one day, I looked up.
And I was alone on the battlefield.

## The Moment I Defected

It wasn't some explosive moment. No cheating. No public scene. Just a slow splintering. One day, I was irritated. We were mid-conversation and he was doing that thing again. Cold. Flippant. Unreadable on purpose. Out of exhaustion, I said it: "Okay, gremlin." It slipped. A jab. Not premeditated. Just a tired woman releasing steam through a smart mouth.

What shocked me wasn't that I said it. It was how he responded. He told me he wouldn't tolerate disrespect. Said he had too much on his plate. Said he couldn't have a woman who tore him down with words. That verbal disrespect was a hard boundary for him. And something about that? Snapped me awake. Because *that* was the line? Not the months of distance.Not the missed birthdays. Not the nights I cried myself to sleep, feeling invisible. *This* was the boundary?

And that's when I realized—I had never drawn one of my own.Not really. I had waved mine off. Folded them up like old maps. Made myself an immigrant in the country of *him.* Learned the language. Adopted the customs. Pledged allegiance to a flag that never claimed me. And here he was—acting like a lieutenant. Scolding me for crossing a line in battle. While he stood miles away from the fight, untouched by the blood I shed daily just to stay.

The irony wasn't lost on me. He—who had wounded me so deeply I couldn't tell where his hurt ended and mine began—was now telling *me* about boundaries. That was the moment.The moment I realized the betrayal wasn't his.
It was mine.
I had betrayed my own country.
And the only way back to myself...was to defect.

## The Last Goodbye

The last fight wasn't dramatic. It was quiet.Tired. I asked a question. He answered honestly, but only because I asked. I got quiet.

To him, that silence was disrespect.An attack. Five days passed. No call. No text. And when he finally reached out, it was a half-apology wrapped in ego.That was it.I blocked him. Not in anger. In preservation. I tried to be done. Sat in the silence.Tried to believe it was final.

But the coldness of our ending gnawed at me. So I reached out. We tried again. Briefly. A few bike rides. Some warm nights. Familiar rhythms. Old laughter. But the cloud came back quickly. We were fighting again.

Misunderstanding each other again. And this time, I felt it. Something permanent. One night, I came over. Sat beside him on the couch. There was distance. I could feel it. His friend called—he had to leave soon. He didn't push it back.

I stood up. Hugged him. Waiting.

Waiting for the hold. The squeeze. The pause.

For him to pull me in. But he was still. Cold.Gone.

I cried—quiet, aching tears. My body trembled against his. Still, he didn't move. And when I let go, he let me. No words. No reaching. No stopping me. I walked out. And this time, we both knew—I wasn't coming back.

## The Truth About Letting Go

Now, standing on the other side, I see it clearly. That moment—his stillness, his silence wasn't cruelty.
It was his final act of love.
Because he knew me.

He knew that if he reached for me, if he whispered *wait...*
If he gave me even a flicker of the boy I had fallen for, I wouldn't have left.
I would've stayed. Again.
And he couldn't let that happen.
So, he didn't stop me.

And in that moment, I became Rose. Floating in the Atlantic, uncurling my fingers from his hand. Saying *I'll never let go.* Even as I did.Not because I stopped loving him. But because I had to save myself.

And it reminds me of something else. Something wild. Primal. Etched into the natural world. The way eagles mate in midair. They find each other, lock talons, and spiral toward the earth. A breathtaking, reckless descent. They call it a death spiral.They tumble, twist, plummet.

A test of trust. Of timing. Of survival.

Because if they don't release in time; If they hold on too long they crash and die together. And that's what we had.

A love that locked us in. A love that spiraled. A love we didn't want to let go of.

Until we did.

At the very last possible moment.

Because if we hadn't, we would've destroyed each other. So, for the first time in years, I pried my fingers off of us.

And I swam.

# //Notes App- 2017: Friday Night

It's Friday night
and my baby is lying right next to me.

I trace angles
and linger in places that I know presses buttons.

My fingers slip
and the warm glow from your eyes renders me speechless.

You pause—
And you look at me like you can see the little God in me.

No words spoken.
Just reverent praise
from the worship of your hands on my thighs.

And I know this is... not pretend.
Not that fake shit people spend years in.

Here—
we have minutes we'll relive for the rest of our lives.
Kisses that are slow, deliberate, methodical—
like you're trying to leave me breadcrumbs
to find you in the next life.

I stay hungry for you.
I welcome sleep
because I don't want to keep you waiting.

I'm coming.
I'm waiting.
I'm looking at the clock…
I'm racking my head because—


. . .


It's Friday night
and my baby is lying right next to me.

I trace the angles
and linger in places that I know presses buttons.

My fingers slip…
and the warm glow emanating from my TV blinds me.

Baby is… my Visio remote.

As my surface level is captivated,
I welcome the distraction—
because the person I want isn't here
and we're both pretending the other doesn't know.

The week is over
and I don't have to pretend with anyone between these four walls.

When did we get so good at pretending?

I fluctuate between being perfectly okay

61

and being the exact opposite.

It's like I want to scream
but I don't recognize the voice coming out.

It's like I crave an unconditional love,
but it's weighing on me—
and I'm carrying the burden on my own.

It's Friday night
and I can't touch the person I love
or do all the deep shit I daydream about.

# I'm Fine

Who needs him?
Not me.
Look at me.
I'm good.

I bought my first house without him.
I started sleeping through the night without him.
I stopped blaming myself for the way he left without him.
I remembered who I was without him.
And I will learn how to love again without him.

He wasn't there for any of it.
And he damn sure wasn't there before it either.

Not when I was begging him to hold space for me.
Not when I was crying in the parking lot over some shit he did.
Not when I was sending him five-minute audio messages trying to fix us—
while he was killing me.

Not when I carried the weight of his wounds like they were mine.
Not when he cut me—
and got mad that I bled on him.

*But I guess it's like what Nikki Giovanni said:*

*Because I loved him, I got the least of him.*

You know what?
**TO HELL WITH HIM.**

I didn't need him then.
I don't need him now.

I'm growing beyond this.
I wrote this book.
I turned my pain into pages.
I turned my breakdown into blueprint.
I built something sacred from the rubble he left behind.

I'm going to sit in rooms I once prayed for.
I'm going to speak and be listened to.
I'm going to create, expand, become.
I'm going to heal—
in public and private.

I'm going to travel to places he'll never go.
I'm going to live in peace, in wholeness, in truth.
I'm going to be loved—
fully, honestly, and with ease.

I'm going to be seen in all my humanness—
and still held with care.

I'm going to receive the love I gave out
with both hands,
with my whole heart—
without begging.

Because there's **NOT** a damn thing—
**NOT A DAMN THING—**
he could **EVER** teach me about **LOVE.**

how come he don't want me, man

# RIP UNCLE PHIL

# III

# FUCK HIM

# Certified Crashout

**"Who da fawckkkkkkk do you think I IS?"**
**-Beyonce-**

It was the night before Thanksgiving.
He'd been distant for weeks—quiet, withdrawn, short-tempered. Said he
was "just stressed." Said work was draining. Said he was tired. But I could
feel the distance growing like a cold draft through a cracked door.

I'd asked if he was coming to Thanksgiving with me and my family.
His answer?

"We'll see."

Not no. Not yes. Just that vague, indifferent shrug of a reply.
He said it was work-related.
But my gut knew better.

That day, his energy was cold.
He was barely texting back. Short. Dismissive.
I kept checking my phone, hoping for something to ease the ache in my
chest. Nothing came.

By nightfall, my intuition was screaming—

the kind only women, especially Black women, truly understand.
Still, I held on to hope.

## The Pop-Up

In my mind, I built this whole fantasy. I imagined pulling up late, surprising my man who'd just been down.
We'd talk, reconnect. I'd stay the night.
We'd fall asleep entangled.

Then in the morning, I'd cook the side dishes I was supposed to bring to my mom's. We'd laugh in the kitchen, sip coffee, and it would feel like things were back on track.

That image was so vivid I packed the car at 2 a.m. with sweet potatoes, foil pans, and hope.

But when I pulled into his driveway, my fantasy collided with reality.

There was another car parked in the yard.

## The Discovery

I parked. Walked to the door. Listened.

His voice floated through the door—light, playful.
A tone I hadn't heard in weeks.

He was talking to someone. A woman.

He was explaining why he liked a certain video game character.
The words were harmless. But the intimacy? Loud.

I pulled out my phone and called.

"Who's calling me at 3 a.m.?"
His voice was casual, like I was a wrong number.

Then I heard her say,
"I don't know. That's your phone."

And in that pause, I felt everything.

I called again.
Not for him.
For her.

I wanted her to know this wasn't just some random friend or a spam call.
I wanted her to hear it—to know there was someone else.

## The Confrontation

He opened the door, startled.

"You got a bitch in your house at 3 a.m.!" I snapped, my voice cutting through
the night.

He blinked like he couldn't believe I was real.
"It's just a coworker," he mumbled. "We're just playing a game."

A coworker? At 3 a.m.?

71

He worked the night shift at a warehouse, 3 to midnight.
And now I was supposed to believe this?

No. He was lying.
And worse—he was trying to make me feel crazy for pulling up.

Something in me snapped.

"You really think I'm stupid, don't you?" My words came through a throat full of heat.

"I've stood by you through everything—your depression, your hard days. I've been your peace. Your support. And this is what I get?"

He didn't say much.
He didn't have to.
That's all I needed—my crash out was underway already.

What made it worse—or better, depending on how you look at it—
is that I had never even raised my voice at him before.

I was always calm.
Always composed.

I was Ms. Therapy Betty—journaling instead of yelling, offering space instead of silence.

I literally bought a book on attachment styles trying to decode our dynamic.
Told myself I had anxious tendencies.
Told myself he was avoidant.

Thought if I could just *understand* him better, I could love us into healing.

Instead of standing my ground and saying he had me fucked up and I was sick of this shit—
I kept trying to be his safe space,
even when he turned me into his emotional dumping ground.

So when I finally snapped? It wasn't just loud.

It was *foreign*.

He looked at me like he didn't recognize who I was.
Like he couldn't believe that this version of me even existed.

And honestly? Maybe she hadn't existed—until right then.

Because I had spent so much time doing everything right—hoping that if I was good enough, soft enough, understanding enough, I'd finally be loved right.

That night, I stopped hoping.

I started hollering.

I snatched the key to his house off my ring and hurled it at him.

"Fuck you."


## What They Don't Tell You About Crashing Out

Crashing out? It's not cute.

It's raw.

Messy.
Loud.

But sometimes, that's what liberation sounds like.

We're taught to stay composed.
Keep it cute.
Rise above.

But that night?
I didn't want composure.

I wanted truth.

Ms. Therapy Betty.
Always listening.
Always calm.
Always full of composure.

And here I was—crashing out.

Not because I lost control.
But because for once,
I let go of the idea that being "perfect" would save me.

Ms. Therapy Betty wasn't listened to.
She was taken for granted.

But that night, when I cussed his ass out?
He heard every word I said.

It didn't matter that I wasn't polished.
I was real.

And I'm not saying crashing out is the goal.
I'm saying I had to stop performing peace like it was armor.

Because no matter how quiet you are, how gentle, how patient—
you can still get hurt.

And if pain is gonna come either way?
I'd rather meet it with my full voice.


## The Aftermath


I got in my car. Drove home.
Slept peacefully—for the first time in months.
No tears.
No regret.
Just rest.

I expected to wake up with shame.
To cringe at how loud I'd been.

But I didn't.

What I felt was pride.

I stood up for myself in real time.
No edits.
No shrinkage.
No polishing my pain.

That night, I didn't perform.
I *released*.

## A Crash Course in Self-Respect

That's what they don't tell you about crashing out:
Sometimes it's the only way to break free.

Anger isn't always destruction.
Sometimes it's construction.

It builds new boundaries.
It clears the air.

It says,
"I'm done being quiet."

That night, I earned my certification in the fine art of crashing out.
Stamped. Approved. Released.

And guess what?

The sky didn't fall.
The world kept spinning.

And me?
I woke up free.

Because sometimes the real power move
is showing people exactly how much they've tried you—
and standing ten toes down in it.

If being a crashout is what it took to come home to myself?
Then call me certified.

# //Notes App- 2019: for what?

I need to chill.
Calm down.
Find me.
Without you.
Without explaining myself to you.

Yeah, you do some fucked up stuff—
but the way I currently am makes it worse.

I damn near had a complete breakdown.
For what?
Because I called you and you didn't answer?
Because I thought you were mad at me for trying to help?
Because you told her your situation instead of me?

Like that's insane.
So I drive to your house. For what?
Make myself sick with worry. For what?
For someone who doesn't even know anything has changed?

I can't.
I can't.
I have to get myself together. For real.
Because this shit is ridiculous.

And no, I don't have to respond to him.
I texted him. I called him. No answer.
Why should I rush to respond to a "☺"?

I shouldn't.

I can't even put a name to these emotions,
let alone ask someone to help me hold them.

I need a friend.
Someone to support me while I figure some stuff out.
I just want to be held.
I just want to be comforted.

I've been making rash decisions.
Rash moves.
And I can't justify it no more.

# The Unbecoming of a Bag Lady

*"Can't be a bag lady—Erykah already warned us about that."*

## Packing With Purpose

I hate packing. Anyone who's had to pack and repack a suitcase to make sure everything fits understands my pain. But we all know it's necessary. Whether it's to make room for essentials that make the trip smoother or to avoid getting pulled out of the TSA line and having your belongings picked through in front of strangers—packing matters.

And in a way, that's what moving on from a relationship looks like.

You're packing up lessons, memories, pain, and versions of yourself tied to someone else. But you can't just toss it all in a trash bag and drag it with you. You have to be intentional.

That's what I was doing.

I wasn't shoving my emotions into a trash bag, hoping the weight wouldn't burst at the worst moment. No, I had a good suitcase. Lightweight, roller-style. The kind that moves with you, not against you.

I took my time. Folded things neatly. Packed with purpose. Took what I needed—lessons, closure, self-respect. Left what I didn't—bitterness, regret, the urge to double back.

It was full but manageable. I could zip it closed. Lock it. And for the first time in a long time, I was ready to move forward.

And then, just when I exhaled, just when I gripped the handle to roll ahead— someone tapped me on the shoulder and handed me one more thing.

## The Link

One more thing to process. One more thing to get through.

It was a link to a YouTube video. A simple message. No context. No caption. Just a blue hyperlink waiting to be clicked.

This came over a year after our official breakup. Four months after a failed spin-the-block moment. One that ended with both of us agreeing—silently but loudly—that we were done. Tired of the emotional whiplash of an off-and-on-again love that never knew how to stay.

We ended decently. No bad words. No dramatic scenes. This time, anyway.

The link took me to a documentary. Simple enough. A woman struggling with a chronic illness. I didn't know what it meant. I asked if he had meant to send it to me. He had. He encouraged me to watch it. Small talk was minimal. There was space between us now—clumsy, heavy, unfamiliar. The awkward dance of two people returning to pleasantries after years of being wrapped in each other's orbit.

Hours later, he followed up:
"Did you watch it yet?"

I hadn't. But him asking again piqued my curiosity.
    So I scrubbed through the video, looking for signs, reading between the
lines, trying to decipher the unspoken message.

I asked him directly—was he okay? Was his family okay?
He assured me everything was fine. He just wanted to share the video for a
good cause. A cause I respected.

But something about it still felt... off.

I kept watching. And then, I saw it.
The end credits.
His name.

He was listed as an editorial advisor. A mix of pride and sadness washed
over me. I didn't know this version of him.

Then, I saw the director's name next to his.
And before I even knew, I knew.

I clicked.

Her social media was one click away. And just like that, I saw her at his
family's annual picnic, his distinct laughter in the background. A few more
taps, and there she was—at his house, lounging on a sofa I had helped him
pick out.

## The Gut Punch

Then another post. Another picture.

Them sitting together on that same sofa, laughing, sharing inside jokes.

It was a knife to the gut.

I had already accepted that we were over. But the way the truth found me? It felt unusually cruel. The documentary link, something he was proud of, was a living representation of work they had done together. A project that connected them.

Blindsided doesn't begin to describe it.
It felt like betrayal in disguise. A Trojan horse in the form of a link.

I wrestled with whether to say something. Whether I even had the right to. Whether saying anything would mean I was letting him get the best of me—again.

Even though I swore I was done revisiting the past, there I was pulled right back into it—the familiar spiral of pain, shame, and betrayal.

## The Message

Part of me wanted to pretend it didn't bother me. To just move on like I had sworn I would.

But the other part of me—the part that couldn't reconcile the pain of being forced to let go of someone I once called home—couldn't help but ask.

I needed to know. To hear the words. To confirm the bleak reality.
Late one night, when the silence felt unbearable, I caved.
I poured out my feelings in a sprawl of texts—raw, unfiltered, typed through a throat full of heat.

I said, *"It's not just the link. It's that you knew exactly what it would trigger. And you sent it anyway."*

His response?
Dismissive. Casual. Like a subtle *"here you go again"*—as if the problem was me, not him.

After all the years we spent together—and months apart—he still thought his behavior was acceptable. Like I was the one tripping.

## The Spiral

His last words to me?
**"No, but whatever."**

The anger. The ache. The quiet insult of being minimized—it all collided in a wave that felt endless.

The spiral pulled at me.

I peeked, here and there—enough to sting. Enough to see them building the life I thought I was waiting for.

And me? Alone. Untangling grief that didn't get a goodbye.
After years of love, sacrifice, choosing him over and over again—the realization that choosing myself was what ushered in the end?

It felt like a cruel joke. Watching him build the life he once told me to wait for—but with someone else?

It felt like grief.

A future I had sewn seeds for. Watered. Nurtured. Only to realize the harvest was never meant for me.


## The Return Home


And then came the realization.
I had spent so much time fighting for something that wasn't even there anymore.
I had made a home out of him.

Maybe I was so caught up in the idea of love that I didn't realize I had always been my own home.

I didn't need someone else to fill that void.
I didn't need anyone to complete me.
And with that, I closed the suitcase for the last time.

I didn't need to pack anything else.
I already had everything I needed.
I had myself.
And that was more than enough.

# This Inbox is Not Monitored

---
---

**Subject:** Come Get This Nigga
**To:** karma@universalbalancellc.com
**From:** Me
**Message:**
You see what he did, right?
When can I expect his ass to be dealt with?
Any assistance or advice regarding this matter is greatly appreciated.
Thank you for your time,
Me

---
---

**Auto-reply from karma@universalbalancellc.com**
**Subject:** RE: Come Get This Nigga
Your claim is currently under review.
Please do not reply to this email.
This inbox is not monitored.
—Universal Balance, LLC

---
---

Since they didn't wanna respond to emails, I pulled up to the office.

I walked into the Universal Balance LLC headquarters already irritated. I'd been waiting for this moment for a *long* time, and the fact that Karma wasn't even there?

Typical.

I glanced at the clock. 2:20 PM.
The sign on the door said **Return at 2:00.**

I took a breath. Bit the inside of my cheek. Squinted at the sign like maybe it would magically update. The receptionist looked up from behind her desk with that tired, don't-ask-me expression.

"She might've called out today."

Called out? *Called out?!*

I exhaled hard. Looked down the hall.

Her office door was cracked open. I walked over, peeked inside.

**Empty.**

Of course it was.

Then I spotted someone walking past—young woman, smart twist-out, calm but slightly over it. Her name tag read: **Destiné.**

She gave me that look. That Black-woman-to-Black-woman look. The one that says *"Girl..."* without even opening your mouth.

I was about to roll my eyes when she shrugged and said, **"What? I do my job."**

Then walked off.

And for a second, I just stood there.

Confused. Irritated.
Lowkey defeated.
Like… *so this how it is?*
He out here wildin', and Karma on PTO

Maybe she's working on a bigger case.
Maybe she outsourced me to *Patience.*
Or *Growth.*
Or hell—*maybe she just don't care.*

Maybe Karma work remote now.
Probably got a good benefits package.
Maybe she's salaried and unbothered.
Maybe she's in a meeting with Closure.

Either way, one thing's clear:
**This inbox is not monitored.**
And apparently?
Neither is my justice.

# Who's Paying for Veal?

*Picture this.*

You're walking through the city, the night stretched out before you, full of possibility. You don't have a destination—just a feeling. A sense that something special might unfold if you stay open.

And then you see it.

A new spot. One of those trendy fusion restaurants with an odd, made-up name like *Erneous Qavali*. The kind of place that wasn't there last week but somehow already has a six-month waitlist. The name sounds elite, like something rare—meant for people who know how to indulge.

The menu? A chaotic mix of flavors that shouldn't work together but somehow—on paper—they do. The kind of place built on ideas. Big ones. Ambitious ones. It promises an experience.

You weren't planning on eating here. But something about tonight feels different.
So you say yes.

You step inside. The lighting is low, intimate. The kind of place where time stretches and meals turn into memories. A waiter approaches—confident, charming. He seems sure of things. The type who's used to being believed.

He hands you the menu. No prices listed, of course. Just poetic descriptions and imported ingredients. You skim it.

"The roasted veal is exquisite," he says, eyes warm, voice smooth.

It's not what you'd normally order. You hesitate.
But something about the way he says it... silences the voice in your head that usually asks more questions.

Tonight feels special. Tonight, you're saying yes.

So you do.

And when it arrives—lord, it's beautiful. The veal glistens under candlelight, seared just right, tender enough to cut with a glance. The flavor? Rich. Complex.

Almost intoxicating.

You've never had it before—and now, you can't imagine *un*-knowing its taste.
    You savor it. You don't rush. You let yourself indulge.

And then— the bill comes.

You weren't thinking about the bill. But now, reality sets in. You scan the list, eyes skipping over the apps and sides, until they land on it.

**Roasted Veal ... $143.**

Your stomach tightens—not from the meal, but from the price.
You look back at the menu. Wondering what you missed. Wondering how you didn't see this coming. But there was no fine print. No asterisk. No

hint.
Just a moment that felt good—until it was time to pay for it.


## The Bill Comes Due


I didn't lose everything—but I didn't walk away untouched.
Some parts of me?
Changed forever.
The girl who thought love should hurt to count.
The softness I handed over too freely.
The voice I silenced to keep the peace.

I paid for that.
In time. In tenderness.
In versions of myself that don't exist anymore.
But even with all that—I tasted something new.
Something rich.
Something rare.

And now?

I don't need the restaurant.
I don't need the waiter with smooth lines or the table that made me wait to
be fed.

Because now?

I cook for myself.
I know how to season my own joy.
I make something better— with my own hands, in my own kitchen,
with peace in the background.

So yeah…I paid for Veal.

But baby?
Now I feed myself.
From a menu with no hidden costs.

# Hello Barbara, This is Shirley

## VERSE ONE: WOMAN TO WOMAN

Hello Barbara. This is Shirley.
*Woman to woman.*
That's a phrase so many of us understand without explanation.
The phone.
The pause before the voice.
The ache in your chest that says, *"This isn't just about him—this is about us."* Whether you've been Shirley. Whether you've been Barbara.

Or maybe you were the friend who found the number and said,
"Girl... you need to call her."
You know.
You know what it means to extend a shaky kind of grace.
To say *I see you* in the midst of being unseen.
To hold the phone like a lifeline. Like a weapon. Like a prayer.

It's not always about warning her.
Sometimes it's just about saying *do you feel me?*
Because deep down, we all know what it's like to be picked up and dropped off in love.
To be deceived, dismissed, or displaced—and expected to just keep moving.

There's something uniquely cultural about that quiet bond between women in pain.
You don't have to like her.
You don't have to agree with her choices.
But you know what she's feeling.
And sometimes, that's all that matters.
But let's be clear—this chapter isn't about her.
This is about me.

Because the deepest betrayal I lived through wasn't what someone else did to me.
It was what I did to myself. Again and again, in the name of love.

I had a whole catalog of betrayal.
Some came with screaming matches.
Some came with tears.
Some came with me texting women at midnight.
Some came with silence.

But the worst ones?
They came with a smile.
Me, smiling through the ache, convincing myself that our love was still worth defending.
I wasn't just fighting for him.
I was fighting to prove that I hadn't wasted my time.
That I hadn't been fooled.
That I wasn't the kind of woman who gives all of herself to someone who didn't deserve it.

I loved him in ways I had never loved myself.
And *that* was the real betrayal.
That I stayed after I knew.
That I made peace with crumbs.

That I abandoned the woman who tried to warn me.

## INTERLUDE: THE FOG(I Didn't Want to Write This)

I almost didn't write this chapter.
Not because I didn't know what happened—but because I did.
I lived it. I buried it. I tried to forget it.
And digging it back up felt like reopening a wound I had just stopped bleeding from.

This was one of the hardest chapters to write—
Not because of what he did, but because of what I let happen to me.
Because I betrayed the girl I was becoming...
For the sake of being loved by a boy who was never ready for all of me.

Some of this is still blurry, if I'm being honest.
Not because it wasn't real—but because I was moving through it in a fog.
That kind of pain lives underwater.
You remember it in flashes.
In sounds.
In pressure.
But not always in order.
Not always in words.
Some of it still lives at the bottom of me—like silt in a jar that only stirs when I try to explain it out loud.

Still, if I leave this part out, I'm not telling the truth.
And if I've learned anything by now, it's that silence never saved me.

# VERSE TWO: THE LIE THAT SPLIT ME

We had just come off a "good run."
Those quiet weeks where things felt easy again.
Where it almost made me forget how rocky we had been before.
But even in the middle of our so-called good—something felt off.

Phones flipped face down.

Stories shifting slightly over time.

Little slip-ups in the details—like he'd told the same story to more than one person and couldn't keep track of who he'd said what to.

The kind of clues you don't want to believe.
The kind of instincts you try to talk yourself out of.
Until the truth refuses to be ignored.

Amazon packages arriving with a woman's name on them—a coworker, he said, who was just using his Prime.
The way he brushed it off so casually made me feel like I was crazy for even asking.

And then came the night I went through his phone.

And that? That was the earthquake.

Everything I had suspected—confirmed.
Messages.
Pictures.
Whole conversations stretching back months.
Maybe even years.

And not just one woman.
But one main one.
A woman deep in it.
Calling him *baby*,
Talking about shared dreams, shared futures—
Like they were building something.

It shattered me.
I broke up with him.
We separated.
For months, maybe two or three.
Then we started talking again.
Slowly. Carefully.
Like trying to tape together shattered glass and convince yourself it's still a window.

He acted like he wanted to do better.
And I wanted to believe him.

So I had a conversation with him.
A very clear, grown, heart-on-the-table conversation.
I said, "If we're really going to try again, you need to handle what's in the background. You have until this date. By then, I need to know that you've closed the old doors so we can open something new. Otherwise... we're done for good."

He looked at me and nodded.

Quiet. Knowing.

And then came that hush before the storm. That "clearing it up" season.
That space I gave him—trusting that he'd make it right behind the scenes.
I gave him a timeline.

Four months.
Told him that after my 28th birthday, I wanted us locked in.
No more "almost." No more chaos.
Just clarity. Commitment. Truth.

I told him, either get right—or we wipe our hands clean and say maybe it's just not us.
And he said that was fair.
Said he understood.
Said we'd be on the up and up.
So I believed him.

We celebrated my birthday weekend like we were turning a page.
New chapter. New us.
He held me. Kissed me.
Said all the right things.
And I wanted to believe it was real.

Little did I know, later that night, the betrayal that would tip everything over was pickles.
Yes.
You read that right.
**Pickles**.

While we were out at a cute little video game dining spot, spending quality time, he stepped away to take a "quick call."
Said it was a friend asking about something harmless.
He was gone for exactly 3 minutes and 24 seconds.

My body knew before he ever came back to the table.
I smiled.
Laughed.

Tried to enjoy the rest of the night.

Because I had promised—after this timeline, I'd be better too.
No more detective girlfriend.
No more pop-ups or crash outs.

But I also knew…when he fell asleep, I was going through that phone.

And I did.

And of course—it was her.
The Amazon Prime coworker.
The one with the packages.
She was the one who called during those 3 minutes.

And buried in their thread,was the moment that changed everything.
A pregnancy test. From her to him.
Her saying she wasn't sure if he was the father.
And him—joking that he'd stock up on goods and snacks for her.

A few days later, a photo.
Sent from him to her.
A giant jar of pickles.
Just like he promised her.
It wasn't just betrayal.
It was *intimate*.
*Deliberate.*
*Insidious.*

Something about those pickles broke something in me.
The care. The thoughtfulness. The familiarity.

While I thought this weekend was a celebration—the start of something new little did I know, it would be our funeral.

Those messages.
The pickles.
All took place days before our celebration weekend.
He had known the whole time.

I collapsed. I screamed. I told him to get the fuck out.
And then, somehow, we ended up on the floor—sobbing into each other's
arms.

Because we both knew, after that night, we would never be the same.

Something inside me broke wide open that night.
Something I could no longer push down or pretend away.
He blamed me for being colder after that.
He said I didn't treat him the same.
He said I made it hard to heal.

But the truth?
I had a baby now.
Not a literal one.
But a version of me that I had just birthed through fire.
She was raw. Untouched. Wide-eyed and wary. And she was mine to
protect.

## OUTRO: I CHOSE HER

By the end, it wasn't just the betrayal that changed me.
It was what it forced me to birth.
A version of me that didn't exist before the lies.

One that wasn't built for begging or bargaining.
One that came out of the fire with soft eyes and sharp memory.

She was new.
And she needed me.
She needed my attention. My protection. My voice.
She needed to be raised in peace—not raised in the same chaos I'd just crawled out of.And I knew then… I couldn't keep calling.

Couldn't keep replaying scenes, rewriting endings, or reaching out for understanding that would never come.

Because while he was waiting on a paternity test…I was already somebody's mama.

And she looked just like me.

So I put down the phone.
Not because I had nothing to say, but because I finally had something to save.

And the next time the phone rang?
Maybe it wasn't even him.
Maybe it was just the ache.
The echo of an old pattern pulling at my ribs, asking if I really meant it this time.

But either way?
I didn't answer.
I wasn't in the mood.

# Hang Up on You. Not in the Mood.

## The Sound That Says It All

Doop doop doop — the classic iPhone hang-up sound.
We all know it. That soft, simple click that signals: *The conversation is over.*
It's quick, unassuming. But depending on the context?
That sound can hit like a slap.

Picture this: you're mid-argument, finally about to land the point that's been simmering in your chest—only to hear it: *doop doop doop.*
The other person's already hung up. You're left holding the sentence. The feelings. The rest of you. It's enraging.
Sometimes traumatic.
It carries the weight of unfinished business.

But here's the thing: Apple didn't have to include that sound. They could've let the call end silently. No ceremony. No punctuation.
But they chose that tiny audio note. A digital door slamming shut. A boundary disguised as a sound.
And lately? I've started to take that sound seriously—not just on the phone, but in life.

## The Power of Hanging Up

Think about it: how do you doop-doop-doop people in real life?
When someone tries to jar you, drain you, disrupt your peace—what's your response?
Because sometimes, the most radical thing you can do is end the call.
Say nothing else. Just click.
Just *doop doop doop.*

It's more than a sound—it's a practice.
A lifestyle. A boundary. A declaration: I'm not in the mood.
Especially for Black women, choosing to hang up is nothing short of revolutionary.

Because historically?
We haven't been the ones to hang up.
We've been the ones getting disconnected from.
The ones left mid-sentence.
The ones holding the weight of conversations that never served us in the first place.

## Receipts from the Line

Let's run the tape.
Black women have always shown up—for everyone.
We've organized. Voted. Marched. Built. Rallied.
We've been the backbone of movements—the scaffolding of progress—only to be shut out when the rewards were handed out.
We marched for suffrage, too.
But in 1920, only white women got the vote.

We had to wait 45 more years.

Or look at the Black Lives Matter movement.
Founded by Alicia Garza, Patrisse Cullors, and Opal Tometi—three Black women.
They gave language to our rage and a platform to our pain.
They built a global movement.

But as the fight grew, their names faded.
Their leadership was questioned.
Their labor was co-opted.

Even in movements we birth.
Even in households we hold down.
Even then—we get muted.

And when we *do* speak up—when we dare to name our pain and demand more—we're called "angry."
Dismissed. Labeled. Silenced.
So when I say hanging up is revolutionary, I mean it's a rebellion against that legacy.
It's reclaiming our right to walk away.
To say: Not today. This is not mine to hold.

## Transmutation Is Tradition

But even when we hang up, we don't walk away empty-handed.
We take the fragments—the disrespect, the betrayal, the weight—and we transform them.
Like we always have.

Black women are transmuters by nature.

We turn scraps into sustenance. Pain into poetry. Burdens into brilliance.

Transmutation isn't a moment. It's a rhythm. A method passed down in our bones.

Take soul food.

More than cuisine—it's a legacy of survival.

Okra, yams, black-eyed peas, collard greens—these weren't just ingredients.

They were resistance. A rootedness.

Enslaved African women braided rice seeds into their hair—carrying nourishment, memory, and culture across the Atlantic.

We didn't just survive.

We carried ourselves into new soil—and made it sacred.

Even our nourishment was a protest.

Even our food said: *You cannot erase me.*

### Resistance Wrapped in Fabric

This power of transmutation didn't stop in the kitchen.

It touched every part of our identity—even our hair.

In 1786, Louisiana passed the Tignon Law, forcing Black women to cover their hair with headscarves, hoping to make us disappear.

They said our styles were "too elaborate," too elegant—too much.

But what did we do?

We elevated the tignon.

We wrapped our hair in bold fabrics, feathers, jewels.

We turned oppression into expression.

Fashion into rebellion.

Our resistance was so undeniable that even Empress Josephine, wife of Napoleon Bonaparte, copied the style.

We weren't just wearing fabric.

We were sending a message.

## The Skyscraper Sisters

That same spirit lives on today.
Movements like the 92%ers are not just about showing up at the ballot
box—they're about how we choose to show up for *ourselves*.

In the 2024 election, 92% of Black women voted.
Again.

But now?
There's a shift.
We're no longer defining ourselves by how much we can carry.
We're asking where our energy deserves to go.

And sometimes, that looks like intentional absence.
Like in Navi Robins' art piece, *Sometimes I Told You So, Just Ain't Enough*—
four Black women sit on a skyscraper, sipping coffee as the city below burns.
They're done explaining.
They're done bleeding.
*They're just sipping their coffee.*

*Doop. Doop. Doop.*

## The Final Click

We've taken the lesson of that little sound to heart. Whether it's walking
away from a draining relationship, stepping back from a cause that no longer
feeds us, or simply protecting our energy from constant demands.

We are hanging up.

We are choosing ourselves.
We are no longer afraid to disconnect.
To step back.
To be done.

Because now we know...
**The revolution will be doop doop dooped.**

\*\*\*

## QUESTIONS TO SIP ON

- What conversations—literal or metaphorical—do you need to hang up on right now?
- Where in your life can you practice active rest as an act of resistance?
- How can you start to transmute the challenges you face into something that nourishes your soul instead of depleting it?

# Niggas Need To Die

I hope you ready to die bout that dick cause I'm ready to go to war for it
-Black Internet-

Some truths don't come with trigger warnings.

Yeah. I said it.

But walk with me for a minute.

I was watching this supernatural show one day — something fantasy, with demons and underworlds. The main character had found themselves in Hell, trying to rescue a loved one, and they had to navigate layer after layer of darkness to get there. But what stuck with me wasn't just the plot —it was the *background.*

The prisoners.

They were locked in cells like a regular jail. But the demons guarding them weren't just standing around — they were feeding.

Feeding off the prisoners' pain.

Every scream, every breakdown, every cry for help made the demons stronger. The more the humans suffered, the more the demons thrived.

107

And something in me clicked.

These niggas are demons.

Okay — maybe not *all* of them.

But I realized I've come into contact with some real dark energy wearing cologne and fresh kicks. Not cartoon villains. Not innocent clowns. I'm talking about men who harm on purpose.

Men who feed off your softness, your confusion, your ache. Men who get *full* off of watching you unravel — and smile in your face while they do it. I used to believe — like a lot of women — that men didn't really know what they were doing. That it wasn't malice, just immaturity. And if not that then at the best of it carelessness and inconsideration and at the worst of it, sheer stupidity. But the more I experienced, the more I *watched*, the more I understood. They know.

And the harm is *intentional*.

I picked up work at this concert series — a little side money. A beautiful gig on the surface: string lights, live music, romantic vibes. Date night dreams.

At first, I looked around and thought, *Wow, look at all these people in love. Look at all these folks who found their person.*

But over time, the veil thinned. And what I saw underneath, cracked me open. I'd take pictures of couples — the guy hugging a woman's belly, forehead pressed to hers, the picture of tenderness and anticipation. And then, as I'm snapping the photos, I'd see his phone light up. *"Miss you, baby 💋."* From someone else.

I was literally documenting the illusion while the truth buzzed through his pocket.

Other times, I'd compliment a couple — literally so drunk in love I couldn't help but to innocently ask how long they'd been together. Only for the woman to say, *"Well technically — we have to wait till he divorces his wife"*.

And then there were the women who showed up at the gates — quiet, standing alone, scanning the crowd.

They weren't there for the music. They were there to confirm something.
They'd seen a ticket confirmation come through his email.
A date he never mentioned.
A plan he never explained.
Now they were just trying to match suspicion to a face.

And then there were the ones invited by my male coworkers.
Every other week, a new woman would arrive.
Different name, different lipstick, same energy.
That look in her eyes — soft, hopeful — like maybe *this* was something.
Like she thought she'd been chosen. Like she thought this man might actually be *different*.

I could always tell.
That floaty feeling. That *"is this the beginning of something real?"* glow.

But I knew better.
Because I'd seen that man here two shows ago — with someone else.
Same body language. Same compliments. Same easy smile that said *you're special* even though she wasn't.
It wasn't just one type of man either. I saw it with the white ones, the Black ones, the ones in suits, the ones in sweats.

Different faces. Same patterns. Harm dressed in romance. Lies dressed in love.

And I'd look at these women — smiling, done up, basking in what they *thought* was affection — and I'd feel it in my chest.

I had been her.

The woman soaking in something that felt beautiful, not realizing disrespect was already seated at the table with us.

I've been the one thinking, This could be it, while someone else already knew it wasn't. There's a certain kind of harm that only reveals itself later — the kind that doesn't bruise until after you leave.

The kind that looks like love while it's happening.

But really?

It's a feeding.

# THE GIRL IN THE TRUCK

Post-relationship, I found myself trying to figure out what dating even looked like for me. I had been entangled with one person for so long, I didn't know how to fully open myself up to anyone new. But a little flirt here and there? What's the harm in that.

I ended up in a brief flirtationship with a coworker. He was younger than me, which already had me in a *"yeah, absolutely not"* mindset. We worked together for a while, and aside from the occasional compliment, a hand that lingered a little too long on mine, or that unnecessary slide-by where he placed his hands on my hips — it stayed surface. A little excitement at work that made the shifts move faster.

And honestly? I was fine with that. I was still untangling. Still finding myself.

But one night, that shifted.
He asked if I could drop him off at his car after our shift. I said sure. On the way, he asked if I wanted to grab a bite. Again — what's the harm? I said yes. I had no expectations. Just dinner with a coworker.

But I can't lie — he was starting to impress me. He talked about wanting to travel and see the Seven Wonders of the World. He was planning a trip to Rio. He was a musician. An actor. He had passions. And that intrigued me.

We got to the bar, ordered food, and somehow ended up talking about our *white girl playlists* — the songs by white artists we play in the car when we're alone and sing word for word like our lives depend on it. I told him one of mine was "Doomsday" by Lizzy McAlpine.

He excused himself to go to the bathroom. And while he was gone, *my song* started playing overhead.
I looked around like *what are the odds?*
When he came back, I was like, "Oh my God, this is the song I just told you about!"
He smirked and said, "I know."
Turns out, he downloaded the jukebox app, paid for a credit, and queued the song — just to play what I had casually mentioned I loved.
I didn't fall in love, but I'll be real: that moment felt like something.

We kissed for the first time that night.
After that, we'd steal a few kisses at work.
Touches, here and there.
But eventually, we slipped back into professionalism. No harm, no foul. He was younger. It wasn't that deep. I was already in love with my solitude anyway.

Then one night, we worked together again. We hadn't seen each other in a while, but the rhythm was still there. At one point, I asked him if he needed something. He said, "Yeah… you." And then later in the shift, caught me in the back room and kissed me like it was the only thing on his mind. He caught me again later on, nuzzling behind me asking if he could come to my place after work.

I told him it was that time of the month, even though it wasn't because although the kisses were nice, I wanted to leave it there for the night.

When the night wrapped, the only thing left was unloading the materials at the storage unit. Before I left the venue, he was closing the truck and stating, Meet me at the storage unit. I said yea, see you in a bit.

I drove straight there.
And as I pulled in, so did he.
With a beautiful woman in the passenger seat.
And that's when it hit me.
This man had picked me to feed off of. I was on the menu tonight.

I saw it for what it was.

He built up an entire evening of work of touches, kisses, asking to come over only to pull up with a woman to try to humiliate me. Completely unprovoked. And here's the thing, not even the dumbest of men would have slipped up in that way. This was intentional.

He could've done a million things differently.
He could've told me not to come.
He could've unloaded alone like he'd done countless times before.
He could've picked her up after.
But he didn't.
He told me to come.

And then he brought her with him.

And she was dressed.

Beautiful. Hair done. Makeup set.

Like she'd just come from an event. Because…turns out, she had.

He had invited her to the concert that night. Unbeknownst to me at that time.

While she was sitting in the audience, enjoying the night he planned for her, he was in the back room kissing my lip gloss off and asking if he could come over later.

The timing wasn't lost upon me either.

He pulled in right before me.

Which means… she was already in the truck.

Waiting.

Sitting pretty in the passenger seat, unknowingly used as part of a setup designed to harm another woman.

Like this was how the night was always going to end.

He planned it.

Every piece of it.

The kisses. The flirtation. The invitation. The overlap.

And then the final blow — making sure I saw it.

Like, *you thought you were special, huh?*

But what he didn't realize was: I'd already seen him. Before he ever pulled up. Because the moment I watched that show — the one where the demons fed off pain — I got the download. That some people don't harm you by accident. They harm you to eat.

And the moment he pulled in with her, I recognized the hunger.

But here's the thing: When you know what you're dealing with, you can move differently. You can't fight demons you can't name. But he didn't

113

count on me knowing his name already.

I knew what I was looking at. I didn't need a breakdown. I didn't need closure. I didn't need a speech. No need for an explanation. No need for "clarity." I already knew the why behind the what.


So I gave him nothing.
No reaction.
No energy.
Not even eye contact.
I simply walked over and started unloading the truck.

There ended up being a problem with the unit — he couldn't get it open, so he had to take the truck back with her still in the passenger seat. Plans: derailed.
I helped him reload every item. Still didn't say a word.

And when the last thing was in, I turned, walked to my car, and drove off.
No "goodnight."
No performance.
No energy to feast upon. The kitchen was closed.
I saw him shaking his head in the rear view mirror as I pulled away.

And as I pulled off, all I could think about was her.
The girl in the truck.
How she was smiling.
How she had no idea.
The light in her eyes. The joy of just riding along somewhere with your man to be when everything feels like a promise.

I thought about how long she took to get dressed.
To do her makeup. To look beautiful to come to an event he invited her to,

while unbeknownst to her he was in the back room kissing another woman. I felt like the all knowing narrator in a book. The one who already knew how the story ended.

But yet… here she was. Sitting in the passenger seat. Grinning. Waiting.
In her chapter 1. Caught up in the rapture.
Just like the the earlier version of myself.
The girl who believed in love so hard it rewrote the laws of gravity.
Who mistook charm for character. Intensity for intimacy.
Who swore what she had was different because it felt like a promise.

But sometimes the harm doesn't show up with sirens.
Sometimes it pulls up in a come ride with me while I do this thing for work real quick, smooth as a smile.

The betrayal isn't just *what* they did. It's that you became a character in their story with no say in the plot. On the road to an unsuspecting end and a weird feeling of why people are looking at you as if they feel bad for you and are are trying to warn you all in one. Sometimes the realization of the part you played in their story comes way later.
After you've pledged your loyalty.
After you've laid your body down like an altar.
After you've swallowed the narrative whole.
And the worst part?
I had been the girl in the truck.
Just in another story.

And just like I have my story, and that girl that night has hers, how many other women have been the girl in the truck?

And this is what I mean when I say…

**NIGGAS NEED TO DIE.**

Not literally.
But metaphorically.
Spiritually.
Egoistically.
Because the version of manhood that so many of them cling to?
That "get her before she gets you," "play the field," "she knew what it was,"
"women are disposable" version?

It has to go.
That mask. That performance. That persona?
That's the thing that needs to die.
And it reminded me of something Jay-Z said on *4:44*.
He said he had to kill Jay-Z — the persona — to be able to love Beyoncé
right.
He had to let go of the man who thought power meant secrecy.
The man who couldn't cry.
The man who mistook pain for protection.
The man who almost went Eric Benét.
The man who finally understood:
To reveal himself was to heal himself —and to heal himself, he had to kill
himself.

Some men make it all the way to the ledge.
They hold the truth like a loaded gun.
And they aim it right at the part of themselves that can't love —
the ego, the mask, the monster they've been feeding.

Some pull the trigger.
But for others?

The gun jams.

And that pause is just long enough for them to climb back down.
These are the men who know just enough therapy language to sound healed.
Who think not cheating makes them exceptional.
Who perform vulnerability but still weaponize softness.
They didn't jump.
They didn't die.
They just got better at bleeding on people and calling it intimacy.

In Black culture, the saying *ride or die* is nothing new. For a while, it's been the telltale sign of struggle love — a relationship where the woman is usually the one enduring. Hanging onto the beauty of the early days, caught up in the rapture, while being actively fed on.

But after experiencing a long relationship that subscribed to that story, I came to a realization:It was never *ride or die*.
It's *ride and die*.

Because when you've been with someone long enough, it's not a question of *if* something will have to die — it's a matter of *what*.
Will you die for each other?
Will you kill the parts of yourself that are harmful in order to grow?
Or will one person die slowly, in silence, so the other can stay comfortable?

And my thing is — is that really asking for a lot?
Because it's not something I haven't done myself.
I've died before.
You already read one of the obituaries.
**RIP Ms. John Redcorn** — remember her?

That was a version of me I had to bury.
A version who loved someone so much she forgot to love herself.
Who stayed too long, forgave too often, and shrank so small she disappeared.

But that wasn't the only death.
Some were quiet. Some were bloody.
Some I didn't even recognize as deaths until years later.

Because women don't always die in caskets.

Sometimes we die in conversations.
In compromises.
In kitchens.
In cars.
In silence.

So what am I actually saying?

I'm saying that in order for us to move forward—individually, in partnership, and as a society—men have to die.

Not literally.

But something in them does.
And not just one man. Not just the "bad ones."
*All of them.*

The whole collective has to undergo ego death.
Because the version of manhood so many inherited—rigid, avoidant, dominant, unaccountable—is no longer compatible with love.

It's no longer compatible with safety.
With connection.
With family.
With future.

They were taught that love is conquest.

That women are rewards.
That softness is weakness.
That being chosen is proof of power—not a responsibility to protect.

Those beliefs have turned too many into demons—feeding off the pain they cause.

Sometimes knowingly.
Sometimes not.
But feeding, still.
And that?
*That has to end.*

Men have to kill the part of themselves that was told it's okay to be unreachable.
That coldness is masculine.That cruelty is charisma. That women exist to be managed, tamed, tricked, or "kept." They have to kill the part that knows how to be performative in public but careless in private.

The part that will call you "baby" while actively breaking your heart.
The part that needs to control women in order to feel like a man.
The part that sees boundaries as rejection.
The part that confuses presence with possession.
The part that believes softness is owed to them—but never cultivated within them.

Because the truth is women have been dying.

We've died over and over again in the name of love.
We've died to our dreams. To our identities. To our instincts.
We've swallowed screams and red flags and full-on confirmations just to keep the peace. We've died in bathrooms with mascara running. In closets clutching our phones. In front of mirrors wondering what we did wrong.

We've buried so many parts of ourselves just to stay.

Just to be chosen.
Just to be safe.
So no—this isn't about revenge.

It's about balance.
About justice.
About mutual death—for the sake of mutual life.

The person who wants to love me now? He has to come to the table already dead. Already stripped. Already decided.

He has to lose the version of himself that's easy to love in public but impossible to trust in private.
He has to die to his ego.
To his desire to dominate.
To the mythology of manhood that taught him he could harm and still be worthy of access. Because he's not.

So many women have walked through their own graveyards, planting gardens on top of where their innocence used to be. We've been through hell and back.

And now?

If you want to ride with me—
If you want softness from me—
If you want *access* to me—
You have to die first.

You don't get to ride unless you're ready to die.
Not just for me.

But to yourself.
To the harm.
To the silence.
To the mask.

This love requires a funeral. This ride requires a death.

**Welcome to death row.**

# IV

# Rebuild

# Why is Soft Girl Life Hard?

"If rest was stolen from our ancestors, then rest will be our reclamation."
-Me-

## The Illusion of Ease

The soft girl life. The trend that took the internet by storm.
Suddenly, everyone was rejecting hustle culture and the "girl boss" mentality.
Gone were the grindset quotes and 5 a.m. wake-ups. In their place?
Skincare, slow mornings, iced matcha, journaling by candlelight.
Romanticizing the little things.
Moving through life with ease.

Easy, right?

Yeah... not so much. At least not for me.

I've always been a busybody—running from one thing to the next, keeping my calendar full like it was proof of my value. And in some ways, it worked. I was sharp. Accomplished. Always moving.

But constant motion isn't the same thing as fulfillment. And it took heartbreak to show me that.

When the weight of grief and disappointment hit, I dove deeper into routines—busy enough to avoid the pain. I kept myself occupied, hoping that if I just stayed productive, I could drown out the grief knocking under all the noise.

Eventually, I thought: *maybe I need a reset.*

*Maybe it's time to try this soft girl life.*

## When Rest Becomes Another To-Do List

I started with the internet's blueprint. Skin routines. Feminine energy. Matching sets. Long walks. Lavender candles. I curated my outfits, perfected my coffee order, journaled in the morning light.
And for a while? It felt like peace.

But before long, it was just another checklist. Another way to perform. Another mask.

I didn't realize I wasn't actually resting—I was still working.
Working to appear calm. Working to seem healed. I had traded hustle culture for aesthetic exhaustion. If I missed part of my morning routine, I felt off.
If I skipped the candles and affirmations, I felt behind.

Wasn't this supposed to make me feel better?

## Patterns Passed Down

I didn't understand why rest felt so uncomfortable until I looked back.
I grew up watching the women around me move. Constantly.
Even on their days off, they were up before dawn—Anita Baker playing while they deep-cleaned the house.
Rest wasn't modeled—it was rationed. A treat saved for the end of a never-ending list.
And that legacy didn't start with me.
It didn't even start with them.

## Rest Was Resistance Before It Was Aesthetic

Black women's rest has always been politicized.

During slavery, our rest was stolen—our labor demanded from sunrise to sunset. We cared for children that weren't ours, maintained homes that weren't ours, worked fields we'd never own. Stillness had to be stolen.

After emancipation, rest remained out of reach.

The Black Codes criminalized unemployment, forcing Black women into domestic labor under the threat of jail.
Even as time moved forward, the world kept expecting us to perform. To carry. To survive.

We were praised for being strong, but that praise came with a price:
Endure everything.
Complain about nothing.
And whatever you do—don't stop moving.

No wonder stillness feels unfamiliar.
No wonder slowing down feels like failure.
No wonder we joke about "Black girl boredom" turning into another degree, another business, another plan—because peace feels suspicious if it ain't productive.

Somewhere deep down, we inherited a belief that to rest is to risk everything.
That if we stop, the whole house might fall.

## When Praise Becomes Pressure

That's why "the strong Black woman" trope is so dangerous.
It masquerades as empowerment—but it's a cage.
It tells us that being strong means being self-sacrificing.
That we are most admirable when we are most exhausted.
But what if that isn't strength at all?
Maybe the greatest act of strength isn't in pushing through—
It's in choosing to stop.

## Rest as Revolution

Rest, for Black women, is not a luxury.
It is not a reward.
It is not an indulgence.

Rest is revolution.
It is a refusal.

A resistance.
A return.
To rest is to reject the systems that benefit from our exhaustion.

It is saying: *I am valuable without performing. I am worthy without producing. I am sacred even when I am still.*

Rest isn't just about what we stop doing—it's about what we reclaim in its place.

Peace. Power. Presence.

And the more we choose rest, the more we give others permission to do the same.


## What Rest Reveals

But rest isn't always peaceful.
Sometimes, it's confrontational.
Stillness makes space for what you've buried.
When I got still, serenity didn't greet me. Rage did.

Rage at what I endured.
Rage at how long I had to keep moving just to survive.
Rage at how many times I pushed down my needs just to hold everything together.

And underneath all that rage—

*me.*

## The Real You

Rest is where you reconnect with yourself—not the version of you that's always performing, always achieving, always checking boxes.

The real you.
The version beneath the titles.
The tasks.
The timelines.
The expectations.

Choosing to rest is choosing to remember who you are when you're not trying to prove anything to anyone.

## A Home Where We Are Free

And that's why rest is revolutionary.
Because when you reclaim your time and energy, you reclaim your power.
You break free from the systems that benefit from your exhaustion.
You show the world—and yourself—that your worth isn't tied to how much you can do, but to who you are.

And when one Black woman chooses to rest, she holds out her hand for the next Black woman to join her in resisting what has been placed upon us for centuries.

We don't just resist.
We remember.
We reclaim.
Together.

We link hands—across skin tones, across regions, across religions, across lifestyles—forming a chain that stretches beyond borders and generations.

Like the Igbo people of 1803, who chose the sea over a life of bondage, Black women will walk into the sea that is rest.

The sea that will take us back home. A home where we are free.

So tell me—what will you choose?

Will you run toward what everyone else demands of you?
Or will you let the sea take you home?

# //Notes App-2019: where's my rock?

I'm realizing more than ever...
I want a man who is present.

No one is perfect but a lot of people are out here seeking perfection.

I want consistency.
I want resiliency.

Someone I can feel safe showing
the worst of my best self
and the best of my worst self.

Someone who is steadfast.
Unmoving.
A rock.

# Bring Me My Purse

**A double entendre if I ever heard one.**

When my mama said it, it meant one of two things. Either our time somewhere had come to a sharp, sudden end—and we were about to make an even sharper exit.

Or—and this was the version that had our little hearts thumping with excitement—she was about to be generous. Handing us a few dollars for the ice cream man.

Two completely different outcomes. But one thing never changed.
The purse always went in *her* hand.

She was judge, jury, and executioner in that decision. Whether she was drawing back or leaning in, it was her call.

Her purse. Her rules.

I didn't know it then, but that was my first lesson in boundaries. In ownership. In power.

And it would take me years—and a whole lot of burnout—to realize I needed to bring that lesson back to myself.

## The Community Purse

For a long time, I treated my own purse like it belonged to everybody.

You need my time? Sure.
My energy? Of course.
My patience, presence, understanding? Absolutely.
No questions. Just "yes," on autopilot.

But here's the thing about autopilot—you miss the warning signs.

Because while I was out here helping everybody else with *their* bags, mine was sitting there, ignored.

And the pilot can't be the flight attendant too.

But I sure as hell tried.

I was flying the plane and running up and down the aisle—passing out peanuts, fluffing pillows, checking seatbelts, making sure *everybody else* was comfortable.

Until one day, I finally sat back in my seat, reached for my own bag.
And realized I didn't even know what the hell was in it anymore.

## The Bag Was a Mess

It felt heavy.
Unorganized.
Chaotic.

And when I opened it, all I found was exhaustion.

The kind of weight that doesn't just slow you down—it paralyzes you.

After spending so long helping other people sort *their* mess, mine looked like a war zone.

And I had no clue where to start.
Small decisions. Big ones. Didn't matter. I froze.
I didn't know I was deep in burnout. Drowning in decision fatigue.
So I did the thing we're taught to do.
I reached out.


## The Support That Wasn't


I had shown up for so many people, I just knew somebody would show up for me.

But when I finally spoke up—when I tried to explain how heavy it had gotten, how tangled and complicated everything was—I didn't get what I needed.

"Damn, that's a lot. Hold on—I'ma call you back."

"Whew, you're going through it! Can I check in later?"

Technically, they weren't wrong.
But it made me retreat.
Because while I was finally trying to make space for *me*, I was being reminded how little space there actually was.

So I pivoted.

I thought: maybe I just need better people. The *right* people.
Folks who care. Folks who've shown up before.

I basically hired a *Board of Directors* for my life—handed them my purse and
let them sort through it.
At first, it felt like relief.
But what I didn't realize was this...
Every time I deferred to someone else, I chipped away at my own self-trust.

## The Erosion

Eventually, I had to ask...
*When did I stop trusting myself?*
Because my life was fine. I was doing well.
But I still felt shaky inside.

I traced it back—to my Bella Swan heartbreak moment.
You know the one.
When the world slows down, and all you can manage through the tears is:
*I just don't want to feel like this anymore.*

When that heartbreak hit, I didn't just lose love.
I lost *certainty*.
I had built my life around beliefs I thought were unshakable:
*This is real. This is meant to be. I'm doing the right thing by staying. This is my
person.*

And I didn't just *believe* those things. I made decisions based on them.
Proudly.

So when it all unraveled—when the betrayal surfaced and the relationship

ended—I didn't just grieve the loss of love.
I grieved the loss of belief.

Because if I could be *that* wrong about something I was *that* sure of...
How could I ever trust myself again?
That was the beginning of the erosion.


## And Still—I Survived


So I overcorrected.
I outsourced decisions.
I deferred to others.
Anything to avoid feeling *that* kind of pain again.

But what I didn't factor in was this:
I survived.
And that changed everything.

Because if I made it through the worst pain of my life—
What couldn't I survive?

The lesson wasn't: *Avoid pain at all costs.*
The lesson was: *Trust yourself to handle whatever comes.*
That was the beginning of getting my self-trust back.

## The Rebuild

Rebuilding trust isn't a light switch.
It's slow.
Quiet.
Intentional.
You wouldn't instantly trust someone who betrayed you.

Why would you expect yourself to?
It takes small steps. Repeated actions. Grace.
Give yourself what you so freely give others.
Stop punishing yourself for what you didn't know.
You don't heal by holding a grudge against yourself.
You heal by choosing to move forward.

Because the truth is—
You're never really single.
You're always in relationship...with *you*.
So treat that relationship like your longest commitment.
Your first love.
Your forever partner.
And build it on trust.

## The Golden Cracks

How?

Start small.

Say you'll do something—and do it.

Drink the water.
Go to the gym—even if it's five minutes.
Take the damn nap.

Every time you follow through on a promise to yourself, you reinforce trust.
And when that trust is rebuilt, everything changes.
You stop fearing failure.
Because you know—you'll recover.
Trust doesn't mean things won't break. They will.
Sometimes *you* will.
But that's not failure. That's being human.

There's a Japanese art called Kintsugi—the practice of repairing broken pottery with gold.
The cracks aren't hidden. They're highlighted.
That's what self-trust looks like.
You don't go back to the version of you before the cracks.
You honor them.
Because the version of you that *exists now*—the one who's been through it, who's had to rebuild—
That version is the masterpiece.

## The Girl Who Believed in Love

For a long time, I thought healing meant going back.
Back to the girl I was before.
But who was she?
Sweet. Hopeful. People-pleasing to a fault.

Believing love alone could fix everything.
If I met her now, I'd sit across from her at a coffee shop.

She'd argue me down, quoting Whitley and Dwayne, romance novels, and the belief that enduring love was the price of a happily ever after.

And I'd just sip my coffee and smile.
Because life will show her. Just like it showed me.
So no—the goal isn't to go back.
It's to become who I am *because* of the pain.
To fill my cracks with gold.
And wear them with pride.


## Bring Me My Purse


Let's be honest—pain sucks.

Nobody wants to be crying in a parking lot, feeling like their chest has a hole in it.

But pain also teaches.

It's the AP class you didn't sign up for—but got enrolled in anyway.
And when you pass the exam?
You walk away with wisdom. With shortcuts. With tools.
The heartbreak. The burnout. The unraveling.
It brought me back to my purse.

And now?
I own it.
I know what's inside.
I know what's sacred.
I know what I'm willing to give—and what's off-limits.

No more autopilot.
No more reaching hands.
No more letting people tell me what to pack.
This is *my* purse.

So when I say *Bring me my purse?*
I mean exactly that.

Whether I'm about to be generous or whether I'm about to *go?*

I got my bag back.

And maybe it's time you got yours too.

# Plastic on the Sofa

Let me take you back for a second—it's '99 going into the 2000s.

Back when summer felt like freedom and joy was simple. Me and my sister would be outside all day, making up new worlds, playing freeze tag and red light green light like we had nothing to lose.

The sun soaked into our skin as we ran barefoot and wild, laughing with no sense of time. We thought we were just playing outside. But looking back, we were already learning rhythm. Learning timing.

Even the plastic-covered couch had lessons waiting for us.

After hours of running around, skin sticky with sweat and feet sore from the pavement, we'd stumble inside—ready to cool off, grab a drink, and crash in front of the fan.

We'd plop down on the sofa, thinking we'd finally found relief—until we tried to move.

**Shhhhlup.**

The plastic clung to our thighs like it had a vendetta.
Every tiny adjustment came with a loud crinkle, condensation building like we were in a full-on wrestling match with the furniture.

It was annoying as hell.

Eventually, one of us would groan, frustration bubbling over:
*"What's even the point of the plastic? What's the point of getting a new couch if we can't even sit on it for real?"*

My mama barely looked up.
*"That's exactly why,"* she said. *"Ain't nobody 'bout to mess up my good furniture."*

At the time, it didn't make sense.
A couch is meant to be sat on. A table is meant to be eaten at. You buy something new to use it—to *enjoy* it.

Right?

But now? I see it clear as day.

That couch wasn't just about furniture.
It was about legacy.
About protecting what was hard-earned.
About preserving what might not be easily replaced.

Because Black mamas?
They always know what they're talking about.
Even when it don't make sense in the moment.
Even when we roll our eyes and mutter, *Now that don't even make no sense...*

And then one day—we grow up.
And the things that once seemed ridiculous?
Start making perfect sense.
Two and two start to look a lot like four.

## What You Protect, Stays

That sofa my mama didn't play about? It lasted.
The same couch that stuck to the backs of our legs, the one wrapped up like
it was too sacred for everyday use, became a constant in our lives.
It witnessed everything—late-night talks, family movie nights, prom dresses,
homework meltdowns, lazy Saturdays.

Memories soaked into the cushions, plastic or not.
She didn't keep the plastic on forever.
At some point, she peeled it off and let us sit freely.
But it lasted *because* she protected it when it mattered most.

"The things that are meant to last—the things that are valuable—can't be left
wide open for anyone and anything to leave their imprint on."

## Boundaries Don't Beg

My mama didn't have to repeat herself.
If she said no food on the couch? We heard it once.
That red Kool-Aid stayed in the kitchen.
We changed out of our school clothes before we sat down.
And it wasn't fear—it was understanding.

Even my daddy wasn't exempt.

I'll never forget when he left a bowl of cereal perched on the cushion like it
paid rent.

My mama walked in like:

144

*"Ced. Get that bowl of milk off my sofa before it spill and mess up my damn couch."*

He groaned.
But he took it to the sink.
Real boundaries don't just exist. They're *reinforced*.
People adjust when you stay firm.
They might groan. But they learn.
They move accordingly.


## Not Everybody Deserves the Back Room

As much as my mama guarded that sofa, we had access.
We knew the rules. We respected the space.
And in return? We got to enjoy it.

But company? They stayed in the front room.
That sofa in the back? That was for *us*.
The ones who lived in that house.
The ones who earned that level of closeness.

Just like not everybody gets to be laid up on your mama's good couch,
not everybody needs to be laid up in *your* energy like they pay bills.
Some folks are front room only.
Smile, nod, serve them tea.
But don't let them near your softness.

We all know what it feels like to let someone too close too soon—
A friend who starts demanding more than they give.
A partner who mistakes access for entitlement.

A coworker who thinks kindness means availability.

Some people want back room intimacy—but only offer front room respect.
And that? That won't work.

## Front Room or Back Room—Know the Difference

The front room is for visitors.
The back room is for family.
And you better know the difference between the two.
We get ourselves in trouble when we confuse who's who.
When we let front room folks lay up like they built the house with us.
When we hand over access to people who haven't earned—or honored—it.

## Some Things Are Just Yours

Funny thing about that couch?
We all had our assigned seats.
And if someone wasn't home, their spot stayed open.
Not because we had to.
But because we understood—some things just belong to you.

Just because you love someone doesn't mean they deserve access to every-
thing.
Some things are *yours*.
And keeping them for yourself?
That's not selfish.
That's sacred.

## Knowing When to Take the Plastic Off

One day, the plastic came off.
No big announcement. It was just… gone.
But by then, we already knew how to move.
We still treated the couch with care. We still respected the space.
Because the plastic wasn't just about protection—it was about *teaching* us
how to protect.

The goal was never to keep the plastic on forever.
It was to teach us how to treat what's sacred.
And when people show you they've learned?
You don't have to wrap yourself in armor anymore.

Because boundaries?
They're not about keeping people out.
They're about knowing who's safe to let in.

And when you finally lay yourself down—soft and uncovered—
It's not because you stopped protecting yourself.
It's because you *don't need the plastic anymore* to keep what's sacred safe.

# //Notes App-2018: putting my pants back on

Honestly, I feel like I'm perpetually the one who cares too much.
It's not just one thing.
Me coming over the last time…
Let's just say it was a long car drive back full of thinking.
And not that you did anything wrong, per se.
You weren't rude.
But I just couldn't help thinking.
And the only way I know how to explain it is through an analogy:
I feel like I take off layers and open up,
dropping piece of clothing by piece of clothing
until I'm standing in front of you—naked.
Completely exposed.
Vulnerable.
Stretched out.
Only to realize that while I've been undressing…
you've been putting your clothes back on.
And now…
I'm cold.
And I gotta warm myself back up.
The only way I know how.
So I'm putting my pants back on.

# Golden Handcuffs

At first, the gold against your skin felt like a promise.
Light. Warm. Deceptively inviting.
It shimmered like proof: that you were chosen. Successful. Enough.

The first pair came after a crossroads in your relationship.
Long after the late-night talks had faded and your shared future started drifting in opposite directions.
But instead of leaving, you stayed.

One evening, beneath candlelight and whispered apologies, a gift was placed in your hands. Golden bracelets. Shimmering with the illusion of forever.

The second pair came from work.
Slipped on quietly after long nights and early mornings.
The promotion didn't feel like celebration.
Just a firm handshake, a title bump, and a raise that made it harder to walk away.

Another set of golden bracelets.
Fastened with congratulations and the quiet expectation to stay.

The third pair? You gave them to yourself.
Not in a single moment, but through small, daily choices.
Choosing routine over risk.

Delaying your dreams until the timing felt "perfect."
Staying comfortable instead of reaching for more.
And you wore them proudly.

Because gold meant success, right?
It meant you were wanted. Chosen. Valuable.

You clung to the weight, believing it was proof you'd done things right.

But the realization came slowly.
Through missed chances, silent heartbreaks, and moments when you barely recognized yourself.

The gold you once adored started to pinch.
The shine reflected all the parts of you you'd silenced to fit the mold.
The bracelets didn't feel like gifts anymore.
They felt like something else.

Something you couldn't name.
Until you looked again, and saw what had been there all along.
**Handcuffs.**
Golden, yes—but handcuffs all the same.
Beautiful enough to make you stay.
Heavy enough to hold you back.

And the hardest part?
You had chosen them.
Accepted them.
Worn them willingly.

Because sometimes, the things that shine the brightest are the very things keeping us stuck.

# We've All Worn Them

Maybe it was a relationship that no longer matched who you were becoming.
A job that offered stability but stifled your spirit.
The comfort of routine, when your soul was craving change.

At first, it feels like love. Like loyalty. Like the responsible thing to do.
But over time, what once felt like freedom starts to feel like a cage.

The question becomes:
How do you know when it's time to take them off?
And what happens when you finally do?

# The Stories We're Sold

Golden handcuffs are often placed on us before we even recognize their weight.
They show up in well-meaning advice.
In cultural expectations.
In every milestone we're taught to chase.

From childhood, the script is clear:
Be good.
Do well.
Find love.
Get married.
Have kids.
Buy the house.

Not just life choices—but proof you're doing it "right."

We see it everywhere.
In fairy tales.
In R&B songs that frame love as something worth suffering for.
In Disney movies where a woman's story doesn't even start until a man walks in.

And now?
It's just evolved.

The "trad wife" movement romanticizes submission.
The "Sprinkle Sprinkle" movement turns love into strategy.
Even in modern spaces, the pressure to meet life's milestones "on time" still screams beneath the surface.

Social media doesn't help.
Curated photos of baby bumps, diamond rings, six-figure jobs.
Reinforcing the belief that success looks a certain way… and happens by a certain age.

But pause and ask yourself:
Do you really want those things?
Or were you just taught that you should?

## Mimetic Desire: Borrowed Wanting

René Girard, a French philosopher, called this the romantic lie.
The idea that many of our desires aren't born within us.
We pick them up by watching others.

When you're unsure what to want, you look around.
You borrow dreams.

You inherit timelines.

Girard broke it down into two types:

- **Internal mediation**: You imitate people close to you—friends, cowork-ers, peers.
- **External mediation**: You imitate people far away—celebrities, influ-encers, cultural icons.

But now?
Social media collapses those boundaries.
Everyone becomes a mirror.
Everyone becomes a model to mimic.
So the real question is:
**Are your desires truly your own?**
Because to break the handcuffs, you have to be honest.
Some of the dreams you're chasing might not be yours at all.

## The Illusion of Security

Golden handcuffs don't just trap you with shine. They trap you with *promises*.
Financial stability.
Emotional comfort.
Social approval.
The unknown is terrifying.

What if you lose what you've built?
What if you disappoint everyone?
What if you fail?
So you stay.

And over time, you don't just wear the handcuffs.
You *become* them.
Comfort becomes a cage.
Fear of change becomes heavier than the weight you've learned to carry.

But here's the truth:
There is freedom on the other side of fear.
Not the kind that confines.
The kind that expands.

In *Lovecraft Country*, Hippolyta—a Black woman who spent most of her life shrinking—finally steps into her power.
She travels through time and space.
She names herself.
In every dimension, she declares:
**I am.**

Two words that set her free.
Because that's what life without golden handcuffs offers:
The right to move.
To shift.
To become—on your *own* terms.

## Real Gold Doesn't Bind

When you finally break free, you realize. They were never gold to begin with.
Just shiny shackles.
Because *real* gold doesn't bind you.
It moves *with* you.

History measured wealth in gold.
But true wealth was never about what you could hold.
It was always about how freely you could move.

Look at Mansa Musa, the richest person in recorded history.
He had so much gold, his travels disrupted entire economies.
But his *real* power wasn't in the gold.
It was in his freedom.

He wasn't tied to one palace, one expectation, one version of success.
His wealth moved with him.
It flowed.
It expanded.
It created.
It didn't confine—it liberated.

That's the difference between real gold and golden handcuffs.
Because real gold was never something to wear.
It was always the freedom to move as you are.

# Mary Bowser

## The Spy They Never Saw Coming

The year is 1863. The Civil War is raging. The nation is split. And Richmond, Virginia—the heart of the Confederacy—is on edge.

Inside the Confederate White House, Jefferson Davis—the so-called president of a crumbling rebellion—sits at his desk. The oil lamp flickers. The air is thick with cigar smoke, sweat, and war tension.

Scattered across his desk: maps, battle strategies, coded messages—the blueprint for the South's survival. Left out carelessly, like no one in the room could possibly understand them. Because in his mind, once he leaves, there's no threat. No one capable of deciphering what's right in front of them. It's safe.

A woman moves quietly through the space—dusting shelves, adjusting vases, hugging the edges of the room like she's barely there. A servant. A slave. That's all she is to him: a shadow. Silent. Unseen. Incapable.

But Mary Bowser knows exactly what he assumes. He thinks she's simple. Illiterate. Invisible unless summoned.

What he doesn't know? Mary Bowser is helping cripple the Confederacy. With every glance, every silent pass, she reads. She absorbs. She commits their secrets to memory with razor-sharp precision. She sees the maps. The dispatches.

The plans meant to preserve their power. And the best part? He has no idea.

Each night, when her work is done, Mary disappears into the dark—back to Union informants—where she recites, word for word, what she saw. What she heard. She redraws maps from memory. Repeats conversations verbatim.

Because of her, the Union stays steps ahead. Because of her, the Confederacy loses ground. And Jefferson Davis—furious and confused—can't figure out why his plans keep leaking.

But the truth? The enemy wasn't on the battlefield. She was right there. In his house.

Because Mary mastered the most dangerous weapon a spy can hold: invisibility. Until it was too late.

## When I First Heard About Mary Bowser

When I learned about Mary, something snapped into place.

Okay—no, I'm not out here dismantling the Confederacy (lol). But the feeling of being underestimated? Of people assuming you're clueless—never realizing you've been clocking them from the beginning? That hit home.

For as long as I can remember, there's been a gap between who I am and how people see me. Maybe it's the masking I got good at—blending in, showing just enough. Or maybe I've just always been layered—an onion of complexity you have to earn the right to peel.

The first layers? That's what people get at a glance—pleasant, grounded, easygoing. And for some—especially men pursuing me—that's all they think there is.

They build their version of me from those surface traits. A woman they can run game on. Someone soft, wide-eyed, easy to fool.

They mistake kindness for cluelessness. Softness for weakness. Quiet for absence.

But here's the truth: I see everything. I see how they see me. I catch the patterns before they even unfold. The recycled lines, the fake intimacy, the calculated interest masked as connection.

"Good morning." "How you feelin'?" "What you got planned today?"

Like those same lines aren't sitting in ten other women's inboxes.
    It's not real. It's performance. A routine.

Then come the sideways comments disguised as guidance: "Hey, you shouldn't do that." "Maybe think about it this way." Meanwhile, they're out doing the very things they try to police me for.

It's all a game—one they think I'm too soft or too sweet to recognize. But the thing is, it doesn't stop in the DMs.

## It's Bigger Than Me

Because this pattern—this being underestimated? It's historical.

Black women have been misjudged, dismissed, and unseen for generations. In meetings. In movements. In strategy rooms and storylines. We've been overlooked and essential.

So many times, I've walked into spaces and felt it happening in real time. The assumptions forming: She must be junior. She's probably here to assist. She can't possibly be the one holding the insight.

That's not insecurity. That's memory. That's pattern.

It's why we know MLK and Malcolm X like the backs of our hands—but not Ella Baker. Not Fannie Lou Hamer. Not Shirley Chisholm.

Even now, it's why Kamala Harris—with decades of public service—is questioned more harshly than men with barely a résumé.

Why? We already know why.

Because Black women are expected to support, never lead. To serve, not strategize. To work in the shadows, while others take center stage.

But the truth? We've always been the ones holding it all together.

Just like Mary. Quiet. Strategic. Unbothered by their perception—because she knew her power.

And that's where the real lesson starts to take shape: it's not just about knowing your worth—it's about knowing how to use that perception to your advantage.

## The Strategy of Playing Unassuming

What Mary did wasn't luck. It was strategy.

Centuries later, Robert Greene would write about it in *The 48 Laws of Power*—Law 21: Play a Sucker to Catch a Sucker—Seem Dumber Than Your Mark.

The idea? Let them think you're naive. Let them believe you're not watching.

Because once people think you're not a threat, they relax. They show their hand.
   And by then? You've already got what you need.

Mary didn't correct their assumptions. She let them talk. Let them leave war plans in plain sight. Let them believe she was incapable.

And because of that? She stayed two steps ahead. Always.

## You've Seen It in Every Heist Movie

It's the classic twist.

The quiet one in the background—the bartender, the secretary, the sidekick—turns out to be the mastermind.

In *Den of Thieves*, the whole movie misleads you. You think one crew pulled the heist—but it's the background bartender who planned everything.

He made the moves. Took the money. Disappeared without a trace.

While everyone chased the wrong people. By the time they realized the truth, it was too late.

That's the power of being underestimated. Not weakness. Not submission. Strategy.

Because when they think you're not watching, they get sloppy. They get loud. They expose themselves.

And by the time they realize you've been studying the entire blueprint? You've already left the building—with everything you came for.


## I Don't Correct People Anymore

I don't explain myself. I don't overperform. I don't audition for roles I already know I'm built for.

Because I know the value of moving in silence. Like Mary Bowser—I make my moves. Quietly. Strategically. On purpose.

Because when you know who you are, there is no title, no room, no underestimation that can contain you.

And no matter how many times we're erased, downplayed, or overlooked— our power remains: sharp. Unshakable. Undeniable. Just like Mary's.

So the next time someone underestimates you? Let them.

They've just handed you the advantage.

Now move—quietly. Strategically. In full power. Just like Mary Bowser.

# Bigger in Texas

You ever be listening to your song—the one that hypes you up, tells you you're that bitch, reminds you you're untouchable, fly, and too smart for the bullshit?

The one that makes you roll your eyes at the thought of being one of those women.

The ones who put up with too much. Who ignore red flags. Who let a dude waste their time.

And then one day... a lyric hits different.

Like—damn. Wait a minute.

Was that... me?

Was I the one acting like a man was a death row meal instead of a charcuterie board? Like my entire future depended on this one situation working out?

Because if we're being real—yeah. At one point? That was me.

That's how I ended up really hearing Megan's song *Bigger in Texas* one day. Not just vibing, but breaking it down.

Because that song? It's a gem.

And that line?

"Y'all hoes treat a nigga like a death row meal, I treat niggas like charcuterie."

That's the one that stopped me.

So let's talk about it.

## The Duality of Megan Thee Stallion

Megan Thee Stallion—born Megan Pete—is a walking masterclass in duality.

She's the balance of power and vulnerability, confidence and transparency. She moves through life unapologetically, but she's never hidden the pain that shaped her.

One thing about Megan—she owns her narrative. She's made history: Grammy wins, industry ownership, cultural dominance. But she's also survived betrayal, public humiliation, and deep personal loss.

And still—she shows up. She speaks up. She keeps going.

That's why her music doesn't just slap. It hits. Because she doesn't just talk her shit—she lives it.

And in *Bigger in Texas*, she's giving us a blueprint. A mindset. A manual for knowing your worth and never shrinking to fit someone else's fear.

Which is why when I heard that death row meal/charcuterie line, I knew she was saying more than just something cute for the beat. She was handing out strategy.


## Let's Break It Down

*"Bet against me, fuck up your parlay / These niggas know I'm the biggest investment"*


This ain't just career talk. It's a mindset.

She's saying: If you bet against me, you lose. Because I'm not just valuable— I'm the main asset.

It's about knowing what you bring to the table and acting accordingly. Not just romantically. Everywhere.


*"Everything bigger in Texas / No injections, we at the pole, no elections"*


This is about real abundance. No enhancements. No validation needed.

Texas becomes metaphor:
   Your confidence? Big.
   Your presence? Big.
   Your dreams? Massive.
   This is autonomy. This is: *I choose me.*
   Not: Pick me.
   Not: Vote for me.
   Not: Approve me.

*"Y'all hoes treat a nigga like a death row meal, I treat niggas like charcuterie"*

This one? Whew. This one is a sermon.

A death row meal is your last supper. Your final joy. Your emotional endgame.
   You savor it like you'll never eat again. Like he is your one shot at happiness.

But charcuterie? That's a vibe. A snack. A choice—not a lifeline.
   It's a whole shift—from desperation to discernment.

From *this is everything* to *this is optional*.
   From "please pick me" to "I'm good regardless."
   You're not starving. You're sampling.
   You're not stuck. You're sovereign.

*"I'm the youngest bitch ownin' her masters / Bitches old as fuck, stuck in a deal, hmm"*

This line is about more than music.

Owning your masters is owning your life—your voice. Your energy. Your time. Your terms.

Being "stuck in a deal"? That's the metaphor for every situation where you give your all and get crumbs. Where someone else profits from your labor, your loyalty, your light.

Megan broke the contract. She reclaimed her worth.

And that's the part that hit me: You don't owe forever to what you've outgrown—just because you once said yes.

*"Y'all gon learn I move on my time / And not for none of y'all amusement"*

This line is about pace. About self-possession. About not rushing your process to meet someone else's expectations.

You're not a storyline. You're not a subplot in someone else's drama. You don't owe anybody a front-row seat to your evolution.

You move on your time. And when you move? It's intentional.

## The Real Message

At the end of the day, *Bigger in Texas* isn't just a banger. It's a blueprint.

Megan is teaching a course in self-worth, strategy, and sovereignty. Here's the cheat code:

- **Know your worth.** You are the biggest investment. Stop letting people who can't see it get close enough to fumble it.
- **Move on your time.** Your life doesn't need a panel of judges. You don't need a timestamp or approval rating.
- **Stop treating men like a death row meal.** That "last chance at love" energy? Retire it. We're in our charcuterie era now—light, optional, well-curated.
- **Own your shit.** Your choices. Your boundaries. Your brilliance. Stop

handing the pen to people who don't know how to write your story.
- **Be loud about it.** Take up space like it's your birthright—because it is.

Megan's not just flexing. She's giving you permission.

To expand. To rise. To move bigger.

Because Texas? It's not just a place. It's a mindset. It's a declaration.

A reminder: Your bigness is not a problem. It's the assignment.

And when you return to your roots—your rhythm—your real self? Everything expands.

Ahhh...

# Harriet Would Have Turned Around

**"I know that I know that I know."**
– Somebody's Grandma

Knowing.
Intuition.
Gut feeling.
God showed me.
I dreamt of fish last night.

You ever hear an older Black woman say something like that—and not question it?

Because you knew Big Mama knew what she was talking about.

The wild part is, most of what they knew? They had no reason to know.

No proof. No receipts. Just knowing.

And they trusted that knowing like their lives depended on it—because sometimes, it did.

We still have that connection. That divine tether. That built-in alarm that's been protecting Black women for generations.

But over time, we drift.
Maybe life beat us down.
Maybe the world got too loud.

Maybe social media flooded us with so many think pieces and "experts" that we stopped trusting ourselves.

It starts as a whisper.

A quiet, *hmm... maybe I should let this go.*

Then you open your phone and get fifty conflicting messages:
"No, sis, give him grace." "Every relationship has challenges." "Actually, leave immediately—why you still there?"

Now you're spiraling. Do you stay? Go? Cry? Forgive? Block? Text *good morning?*But deep down? You already knew. You just didn't trust yourself enough to listen.

## Harriet

Harriet Tubman—born Araminta Ross—was more than a conductor on the Underground Railroad. She was a master of spiritual navigation.

At age twelve, she was struck in the head with a two-pound weight. The injury left her with lifelong "spells"—moments where she'd fall unconscious.

Some called it a disability.

Harriet called it divine conversation.

She didn't just move by map. She moved by knowing.

If something felt off, she didn't wait for proof. She turned around.

She didn't rationalize. She didn't second-guess.
She moved when the spirit told her to move.
How many times have we done the opposite? Felt the shift.
Ignored it. Stayed too long—not because we didn't know, but because we didn't want to.

Harriet didn't wait for danger to prove itself. She trusted the unseen. And that was enough.

## The Prophecy of 2016

Harriet didn't need proof.
But me?

I had the proof before I even knew it was proof—and I still didn't listen.

In 2016, I had a dream. At the time, everything felt fine. No drama. No red flags.

But something told me to write it down.

So I did. Then forgot about it.

Years later, after it all fell apart, I was scrolling my old Notes app, random grocery lists, half-finished to-dos, and then, there it was.

A journal entry from 5:55 AM:

*"I saw a new profile picture of him. The comments were hyping him up—calling him 'the man.' He was in a Waffle House bathroom, and in the background, a girl was ducked off with him."*

*"Another photo: him in bed, grey sweatpants—just like how we used to cuddle. But instead of me, there was a pair of pink shoes."*

*"A comment said: 'Looks like you're missing somebody.' And he replied, 'Yeah... wishing.' With a pink shoe emoji."*

*"Then, I could read his texts. He was telling a girl he missed her. Said he used to play in her 'slightly nappy hair.'"*

I woke up crying.

But I wrote it down anyway.

And years later, when the betrayal came? It didn't match the dream detail for detail—but the *feeling*? The truth underneath? It was the same.

What once felt symbolic had revealed its meaning.

The Waffle House bathroom?
His hidden life.
The pink shoes?

A quiet knowing—someone else would one day take the space I held.
And that fish I dreamt of?

Maybe it wasn't a baby, like the old folks say.
Maybe it was my spirit swimming ahead—trying to show me what I wasn't ready to face.

I didn't know it then.
But I know it now:
My intuition wasn't being dramatic.

It was trying to prepare me.

## The Lesson

I walked straight into heartbreak like someone strolling through a minefield.

My gut warned me.I kept going. And I paid for it—with time.

With grief.
With rage.
With resentment I had to claw my way out of.

Yes, he was wrong. But I was warned. And I ignored it.

Harriet would have turned around.

Not out of fear—but out of trust.

Trust in her gut. Trust in her God. Trust in the voice that said: *Danger is close. Go.*

## This Time, I Did

Months after the breakup, I met a man on the street. Casual conversation. Harmless enough.

That night, I had a dream.

Not a regular dream.

It felt like I was hovering above his life—watching it unfold.
I saw his house.

Not just messy—broken.

The energy felt unstable. Off. Unsafe.

And I knew.He wasn't looking for love. He was looking for opportunity.
I woke up. And I was done. No seeing where it went. No *maybe one date.*

Just—done.

Months later, after I posted about buying my house, he popped back up in
my DMs:
*So are you not interested?*

I didn't respond.
I didn't have to.

I already knew.

Harriet would have turned around.
And this time, so did I.


## The Knowing Is Enough


I didn't wait for pain.
I didn't wait to be gutted open before I moved.

I trusted the whisper.
I honored the warning.

I let the knowing be enough.

Because Harriet would have turned around.
And now?
So will I.

# Girlhood Was Our First Spell

The first spell I ever cast wasn't from a book.
It was handclaps and rhythm on a playground.

*Miss Mary Mack, Mack, Mack*
*All dressed in black, black, black*
*With silver buttons, buttons, buttons...*

Hands slapping. Fingers snapping. Bodies moving in sync.
That was the first time I felt the magic of girlhood.

An initiation into rhythm. Connection. Repetition. Memory.
Before we had language for community, we had games like that—rituals in
disguise.

That's how we learned to move with each other.
To carry tempo and tenderness at the same time.

And if Miss Mary Mack was the first spell, then double dutch was the first
ceremony.

The ropes turning like clockwork.
Girls on either end swinging in perfect rhythm.
A crowd on the sidelines calling out counts, clapping encouragement.

That moment before the jump? Infinite.
A heartbeat of breath and doubt.

I remember standing at the edge, rocking back and forth, nerves buzzing.
Trying to time it just right.
Trying not to trip.
And when I finally jumped in and caught the rhythm?
Magic.
Not just because I got it right—but because *we* did.

The turners.
The rhythm.
The cheers from the sidelines.

We were feeding off each other's energy.
In sync. In spirit. In spell.

That was sisterhood, too.
Before we ever talked about emotional safety or sacred space—we were already practicing it on the playground.

Then, slowly, something shifted.

We went from girls playing in rhythm to girls changing in rhythm.

It started with a whisper.
A girl left school early—jacket tied around her waist.

When she came back, she carried a pocketbook.
Asked to go to the bathroom more.
Moved quieter.
Watched differently.

And one by one, we followed.
Pocketbooks. Pads.
A slow, silent transformation into womanhood.

They call it menstrual synchrony. Some say it's not real.

But if you've ever lived with women, you know—we sync.
In body. In energy. In friendship.

We grow side by side.
We pick up each other's patterns.
And somehow—we don't just become.
We become *in rhythm*.

That's sisterhood, too.

There's a softness in real friendship.
The kind where silence isn't awkward—it's permission.

Where you can sit on the floor with someone who knows your heart, even
when you don't have the words.

Where grief doesn't need to be pretty to be held.
When I was in the thick of it—grief, heartbreak, unraveling—it was my sister
who held the line.

She knew everything.
Not because I performed it for her—but because I didn't have to.

I could hand her the ugliest, most tender truths—and be met with comfort,
not correction.

She was my lifeline.

A place to land.
A place to speak before I had wisdom.

To be raw and unhealed—and still feel loved.

Just the act of sitting next to her.
Crying on the phone.

Hearing her say, "I get it" or "You're not crazy"…
It cracked something open in me.

Reminded me I didn't have to hold everything alone.
That someone loved me in real time—not just in my healed form.

And my girls?

The ones who text back full paragraphs.
The ones who laugh with their whole chests and cry when you cry.
The ones who say, "You bugging—but I get it," and mean both parts.

I've grown through those conversations.
Unearthed things I didn't know were buried.
Been lovingly challenged.
Gently confronted.
Fully seen.

There were moments when my own thoughts turned on me—and they turned me back toward myself.

That's love too.

But it hasn't always been soft.

There are wounds shaped like women, too.
Sometimes girlhood wasn't safety.

It was being left out.
Side-eyed.
Talked about in whispers that never made it to your face.

Sometimes, the rope never slowed down long enough for you to jump in.

We don't talk enough about the loneliness that can live inside sisterhood.
The grief of losing a best friend.
The silence after a fallout.
The ache of knowing the girl who once held all your secrets is now a stranger
with them.

Some of us learned early not to trust other women.
We heard: "I just don't get along with girls."
We watched our mothers isolate themselves out of survival.

We were taught to see each other as competition instead of reflection.

Scarcity got passed down, too.
The lie that only one of us gets to win.
The myth that your softness erases mine.
The belief that closeness always ends in hurt.

But even with all that—even with the ache, the distance, the miscommunication—
I still believe in us.

Because when sisterhood is real—when it's rooted in truth, allowed to bend
and breathe and bloom—it will change your life.

Me and one of my closest friends have this thing we do.

We call it our little podcast.

No mic.
No audience.
Just us.

Episode 237 of something no one else will ever hear.

We spiral.
We land.
We figure it out.

The beauty is in being witnessed.
In being held without needing a solution.

It feels like therapy, but softer.
Like a mirror that doesn't distort you.
A check-in that says, *I see you,* even when you're still foggy on who you're becoming.

There's a healing that happens around grown women who help you put yourself back together.
Women who look you in the eye and hand you truth with tenderness.
Who don't rush you toward peace but sit with you in the process.
Who say, "Baby, I've been there"—and mean it.

Who welcome you into understanding, not like a lecture—but like a home.

They don't always have the answers.
But they've walked enough roads to recognize the signs.

And when they speak, it doesn't feel like advice—it feels like inheritance.

Like they're placing something sacred in your palm.
Something that says:

You're not alone.
You're not broken.
You're just arriving.

And if we're talking about returning to yourself?
Let's talk about Saturday mornings in the hair shop.

When I was a little girl, it was the warm hum of blow dryers and gossip, the
smell of Blue Magic and hot flat irons.

A Black girl's church and therapy all rolled into one.

Now, as a woman, it's tea tree oil and scalp steamers.
Interlock needles clicking in rhythm.

And still—it feels like a place to be made whole.
Inside and out.

What I've learned is this:
Intimacy doesn't only live in romance.

It lives in the voice that says, "Just making sure you made it home."

In the text that says, "I know today's heavy—call me when you can."
In the friend who keeps showing up when life stops being pretty.

And on the other side?
You showing up for them.
Grace for when they're distant.
Patience when they're not themselves.

The belief that love can bend without breaking.

Because we all need to be held.
We all need space to unravel and return.

For Black women especially, friendship is often where we first learn what
we want from love.

Where we whisper, "I want someone to check on me like this."
Or, "I want to feel this safe."

And it's our girls who look us dead in the eye and say:
You're not asking for too much.

Friendship taught me I could be soft and sacred at the same time.
In-process and still worthy of tenderness.

And sometimes?
Love doesn't look like the movies.
No flowers.
No slow fade to black.

Sometimes love shows up in the group chat.
Sometimes it pulls up with snacks and says, "I got you."
Sometimes it sounds like laughter through tears.

Or the voice that says, "I already know. You don't have to explain."
And sometimes?

It just sounds like—
Girl.

And somehow—that's the spell we've been casting all along.

V

Fly

# //Notes App- 2018: once

What does real love feel like?
No hiding. No justifications. Just a statement.
A stand-alone.
À la carte.
Good by itself. Nothing else needed to fortify it.

Why do I do the things I do?
Why do I give you privileges you didn't ask for?
Give you extensions on assignments you forgot were due?
Slash the F into an A before the report ever reaches your fingers?

Why?

Maybe as much as I think it's about you... it's about me.

Maybe as much as I want to give you accolades...
I'm scared of running the race and earning them myself.

Scared.
Fearful.
Excited.
Nervous.
Ready for stage 2.
Not sure where stage 1 ends.

Want to be the definition of a strong Black woman, but in some corner of my mind I still feel like I'm a girl pretending I know the next step.

Pretending like it's gonna be okay because I've seen it a thousand times, watched it a million, but only felt it once.

Only knows what it feels like once.
And scared to admit that once was almost too much.

Once is almost where it ended.

Once.

# Pretty Wings

**"Once you release the shame of being a bird, you'll
remember you've known how to fly all along."**
-Me-

A bird gonna be a bird. And in this case? I'm talkin' about pigeons.

Once upon a time, pigeons were the blue checks of the sky—important, trusted, even revered. Carrier birds. Messengers. They flew across cities and battlefields with secrets tied to their feet, always finding their way home.

They were dependable. Trainable. Loyal. They had a purpose.
Then came technology—faster, cleaner, more efficient. And just like that, pigeons got replaced.

Some tried to go back to the wild, but it didn't go smoothly. After being domesticated so long, they'd lost their instincts. They didn't know how to build nests anymore. They'd pile up a few rocks, maybe some straw, but it was barely enough to hold them. Definitely not enough to protect them.

And I remember learning that and thinking—

See? That's what happens when you take something out of its nature and

try to give it a new purpose.

That's what happens when you interfere, thinking you know better.
I thought I was the one helping—a steady hand offering structure, safety, direction. The one scooping up a struggling little bird and giving it shelter.

But the more I sat with it—replayed old conversations, old patterns—me pouring and performing and stretching—the more it clicked.

I wasn't the rescuer. I was the bird.

I kept thinking I was holding someone else up. Feeding people pieces of myself like breadcrumbs—trying to help them feel safe, feel seen, feel steady. Telling myself I was helping them grow. Helping them love better. Helping them build something real.

But when did I stop trusting myself to just be?
Why was I always flying back to broken places?
Why was I teaching people how to build nests when I didn't even have one of my own?

That's when it hit me:

**Damn... I'm the bird.**

All that time thinking I was the structure—I was the one needing to come home to myself.

Because here's the truth.

When you spend your time trying to help someone "see their potential," trying to lead them out of what you think they've outgrown, trying to build a nest for someone who didn't even ask for shelter—you end up out in the cold, too.

I called it love.
Loyalty.
Being solid.

But a lot of it was me trying to control the outcome—trying to make someone become who I needed them to be, so I wouldn't have to let them go.

I thought I was helping. But sometimes? Helping is just another form of holding on. And holding on to someone who's already showing you who they are? That's not compassion. That's fear.

And then there was him.

My ex.
I had to learn—not everyone is lost.
Some people are right where they want to be, even if it looks wild or unfinished to me. Even if I love them.

You can't save people from their own path. And you shouldn't.
Because in trying to change him, I was changing myself.
Shrinking. Softening my boundaries.
Showing up with love and structure and wisdom—while my own nest crumbled beneath me. I used to say I was just helping. Just nudging. Just supporting him through his learning curve.

But truthfully?

I wasn't letting him take the test.
I was pacing the aisles like a tired teacher—dropping hints, whispering answers, circling the page in pencil.
Pretending I was watching him take it, when really?

I was taking it for him.

We made it all the way to AP-level love—but I was the one doing all the homework.

And not even because he asked. I was just so excited he liked me back.

You know the story—the smart girl doing the jock's assignments.

"Helping," because deep down, she still can't believe he sees her.

That was me.

I didn't want to admit it, but I knew this pattern.

The overachiever. The good girl. The one who over-functioned, over-extended, over-loved—because part of her still felt like that nerdy little girl just happy to be chosen.

I kept calling it love. Support. Loyalty.

But really?

It was insecurity dressed up in responsibility.

It was performance.

I wasn't just helping.

I was auditioning.

Trying to prove I deserved to be chosen again tomorrow.

So when I finally stopped—when I said, *"I'm not giving out answers anymore. Show me what you've learned"*— he failed.

Over and over.

And that's what stung the most.

After all the tests I helped him pass, after all the quiet saving I did—he didn't even recognize it.

I had stepped in so many times, kept things from blowing up, redirected the fallout—that by the time he started dismantling everything, it felt... intentional.

Almost like he didn't care what he lost because he never realized how much had been held together for him.

192

That's the thing about over helping—people rarely appreciate the net you threw under them. Especially when they didn't know they were falling.

And I've learned—especially with men—when you hold them through their hard seasons, they don't always feel grateful.

Sometimes they feel exposed.

And exposure? That's a kind of vulnerability some men don't know how to process. I think at some point, he looked around and realized, "I wouldn't have most of this without her."

But instead of wanting to protect that, it made it easier to walk away. Because sometimes, when people see what you helped them become, they don't feel seen. They feel indebted. And that shame will make them run.

One day, he looked at me and said, *"I just want to start over."*
And for a second, I thought he meant with me. A clean slate. A new beginning.
But what he really meant was—he wanted to start over with someone who didn't know his backstory.

Someone who hadn't seen all the tests he failed.
Someone who wouldn't bring up the boy he used to be.
He didn't want to pass the test.
He wanted to rewrite it.

And when I understood that, something in me finally let go.
I used to think love meant holding on. Meant helping. Meant proving my worth by staying through the struggle—building the nest, filling in the gaps, teaching someone how to love me right.

But now I know—sometimes love is walking away so they can learn for themselves. Sometimes love is releasing someone with compassion, even if they never say thank you.

Even if they never come back better.
Even if you never get the apology.

That's what *Pretty Wings* is about. Not bitterness. Not revenge. But a compassionate goodbye. It's looking someone in the eye and saying: *"I loved you the best I could. And now, I love me enough to stop."*

Because sometimes love isn't enough to make someone ready. And that doesn't make you a fool.

It makes you human.

A bird who finally remembered she had wings.

And yeah... for a while, the hardest part was realizing I had been a bird. Because in our culture, being "a bird" means you were foolish.

Naïve.
Easy to fool, hard to free.
And I won't lie—there was shame.
In how much I gave.
In how long I stayed.
In what I knew and still tolerated.

No matter how far I drifted from myself, one thing stayed true.
Birds have wings.
Which means I can leave.
I can start over.
I am never stuck.

And pigeons?

They weren't chosen for no reason.

They were picked because they have a remarkable homing instinct—the ability to find their way back, even after being carried miles from where they started.

Even when they've been trained to carry someone else's message.
Even when they've forgotten what rest feels like.
Even when they've been told their job is to serve.
They still know how to come home.

And so do I.

And so do you.

So if you've ever been the bird—lost in someone else's story, circling the skies trying to be good, helpful, useful. If you've ever been ashamed of how far you strayed from yourself...

Just remember, you can fly.

And more importantly?

You know how to come home.

# The Grandma Is The Baby

*"The grandma is the baby."*
- Joseline Hernandez-

I once watched a live video of Joseline Hernandez talking about motherhood. She meant to say, "If your mama's the one raising your child, then she's really the mama." But what came out instead was: "The grandma is the baby."

It sounded like a slip. But it wasn't. It was one of those accidental truths.

Because in a way, the grandma really is the baby. Not just because grandmothers often raise their grandkids—but in a much deeper, more literal way.

Before our grandmothers ever held us in their arms, they carried us inside their bodies.
We're linked to them in ways that go beyond stories or warnings.
We're connected in blood. In bone. In biology.

## My Maternal Grandmother

I never got to meet my maternal grandmother.
She passed when my mom was just five years old, so there weren't many

stories to pass down. She was more of a myth than a memory.

I wanted to know her. Not just her name or relation—but who she was.

People talk about their grandmothers like second mothers. How they shaped them. Spoiled them. How they smelled, cooked, laughed.

And I had that, in a way, with my paternal grandma, Mary. But on my mother's side, there was this gap. A missing piece in the puzzle of my lineage.

She only had one photo. I remember the day I saw it.

I'd just come home from middle school crying. Kids had teased me about my dark skin. *Why you so Black? Why you look like that?*

It wasn't just their words that hurt. It was the fact that I felt like the only one. The darkest one in the family. Like something about me didn't belong.

I asked my mom, tears in my throat:
"Why did I have to look like this? Why can't I be regular Black—like you? Like my sister?"

She didn't say a word. Just walked to her closet, pulled out an old album, and handed me the only photo she had of her mother.

"Look," she said.

And I did.

Her skin was deep and dark—just like mine.

"You just like my mama," my mother told me.And I was.

That was the moment she became real. Not just a name in a story, but a woman I carried inside me—and who had carried me.

## Carried in Her Body

That moment sparked something in me. A longing to trace the women who came before me.

And that's when I learned the truth that changed everything. When a woman is pregnant with a girl, that girl already carries all the eggs she'll ever have. Which means that when my grandmother was pregnant with my mother— my mother was already carrying me.

I had been inside her.
I existed within her body.
And she still exists in mine.

Science backs it up. Mitochondrial DNA is passed down directly through the mother's line, unchanged. The same cellular power that pulsed through her body pulses through mine.

We're not just carrying their memories. We're carrying them.

## Warnings from the Women Before Us

But inheritance isn't just biological. It's spiritual. Emotional. Energetic.

Even if I never met her, I inherited her—through my mother. Through aunties. Through strangers at the beauty supply store giving me unsolicited advice that hit too close to home.

That's the thing about our grandmothers:
They warn us.
Sometimes it's soft.
Sometimes it's loud.
Sometimes it's not even in words.

Science calls it epigenetics—how trauma and survival shape the body and can be passed down.

The fear. The vigilance. The instinct to stay small or stay ready—it's not just personal. It's historical.

But just as pain can be passed down, so can power.
So can joy.
So can fight.

Our grandmothers didn't just leave us with scars.
They left us with armor.

## The Secret Check-In

"Get your education."
"Have your own money."
"Don't let no man mess up your life."

Some of us got it soft. Some of us got it sharp.

I lost count of how many older women asked me the same three questions, no matter where I was:

"How old are you?"
"You married?"
"You got kids?"

For a while, I didn't get it.
Why those questions? Why not: "What do you do?" "Where are you from?"

But then I realized—they weren't just curious.

They were checking. Running a quiet scan.

And every time I answered "No," they smiled.
"Good," they'd say.
"Don't rush. Live your life."

Like a secret being passed down. A quiet resistance. A shared prayer.


## The Story That Changed Everything


My ex was close to his great-aunt. He admired her relationship with his uncle—thought it was proof love could last.

One night, he told me a story:
His uncle came out the bedroom, stomach grumbling.
*Boo, I'm hungry.*
She rolled her eyes.
*Now why the hell you ain't fix something yourself? You know I done cleaned this kitchen.*
Still, she made him a tuna sandwich.
He thought it was sweet.
I thought so too—at first.

## The Conversation That Shifted Everything

Later, we asked her how they'd made it 40 years. She told us how she found out her husband cheated—right there in the grocery store.

Locked eyes with a pregnant stranger.

The woman smirked and said, *I'll be seeing our man later tonight.* She stayed. Raised the child. Swallowed the betrayal.

And I sat there thinking: How did she not put glass shards in that man's sandwich?

He walked away thinking, *If they made it, we can too.* I walked away thinking, *God, don't ever let that be me.*

## We Are Not Our Grandmothers—We Are Their Answered Prayers

Men love to say:

"Women today aren't like the women back then."

And they're right. We are not like our grandmothers. We are their answered prayers. They stayed so we could choose. They sacrificed so we could rest. They endured so we could decide. It wasn't that they had stronger values. They had fewer options.

Just one generation ago, in 1974, women couldn't get credit in their own names. No loan. No lease. No life—without a man's signature. So no—they didn't stay because they wanted to. They stayed because they had to.

## We're Also Carrying the Future

If we have children—and if they have children—we'll carry them just as we were once carried. But even if we don't, we still shape the future.

Through the lives we lead. Through the rest we choose. Through the softness we reclaim. We're mothering something.

And it matters. That we choose joy. That we heal.That we live full lives.
Because we're not just carrying the past.
We're carrying what comes next.
We existed inside our grandmothers. And now, they exist inside us.
The same energy that carried them through pain now pulses through us.

But here's the question: If they carried us through hardship—what happens when we carry them in peace? What happens when we are the soft place?

The healed one?
The free one?
Struggle leaves marks.
But so does freedom.

Imagine the genes we awaken when we choose ease instead of exhaustion.
Joy instead of survival.
A full life instead of just a long one.
We are the conduits of our carriers.
And just like they carried us forward—so will the next ones.

So the choices we make now?

They won't end with us.
They'll echo.
They'll ripple.
They'll rearrange the future.
Let's make them count.

# VI

# Bloom

# Don't Wait For Flowers

## My Connection to Flowers

Women and flowers have always been intertwined—blooming, shedding, thriving, surviving. Maybe that's why we're drawn to them.

I've always been a flower girl—very classic, I know. But something about how flowers exist purely for beauty—how they enhance the space around them just by being—has always reminded me of women.

Just by being, we make everything around us more beautiful.

Even when I didn't realize it, flowers kept calling to me.

When I was a teenager, I got the bright idea to get a tattoo. I was instinctively drawn to the fleur-de-lis. At the time, I didn't even see a flower—I saw two C's, our initials, connected by a middle piece. Perfect for a sister tattoo, I thought.

And so, we got it inked.

It wasn't until afterward that I really understood the meaning. The fleur-de-lis—the lily, the iris—has been a symbol for centuries. It represents rebirth.

A new life blooming. Its sturdy stem signifies strength and sustenance.

Some even associate it with the Virgin Mary—femininity, purity, the harmony of divine and earthly.

Without knowing it, I was drawn to something that mirrored everything I would eventually come to embrace about myself.

Years later, during a rough patch—when my long-term relationship was unraveling—I found myself reaching for something. Anything.

Heartbreak and tattoos just go together, don't they?

On a random afternoon, I got up and decided I wanted a side panel piece. Walked into the shop. The hum of the tattoo gun. The sharp scent of antiseptic and ink.

The artist asked what I wanted. I shrugged.
"Anything."
The truth? I wasn't looking for a design. I was looking for pain.
Something sharp. Something real. A sting to cut through the numbness—even for a second.

I scrolled mindlessly, until something made me stop: a flower I'd never seen before.

The moonflower.

It blooms only at night—thriving in darkness, revealing its beauty under the moonlight.

It felt... right.

Spiritually, the moonflower represents mystery. Intuition. Transformation. The kind of beauty that emerges from the dark.

I didn't need time to think. As the needle carved soft petals into my skin, I let the sting anchor me.

Not just ink—release. A physical echo of the ache I'd been carrying.

And without hesitation, I had chosen something that mirrored exactly where I was:

A bloom in the dark.

## The History of Flowers and Women

Flowers have always spoken to women—and not just in metaphors.

Maybe it's because, like flowers, we bloom in our own time. We thrive when nurtured.

Even after we've been cut, we remain beautiful.

This isn't new. The connection between women and flowers goes way back—not just in beauty, but in survival.

In the 19th century, when women's voices were silenced, flowers became their language.

Carefully chosen bouquets carried coded messages—love, longing, defiance.

In an era when emotions had to be swallowed, women used petals to say what they couldn't.

A red camellia for admiration.
A yellow rose for friendship.
A striped carnation for rejection.

Floral prints in fashion weren't just pretty—they were a quiet rebellion. This was the rise of floriography: the language of flowers. Charlotte de La Tour's *The Language of Flowers* became a cultural guidebook, giving women power without permission.

But flowers weren't just soft. They held sharp edges too.

In 17th-century Italy, Giulia Tofana used the belladonna flower to create an undetectable poison that helped over 600 women escape abusive marriages. Flowers weren't just symbols. They were survival.

Later floral dictionaries assigned belladonna the meaning of "silence."

A poetic, chilling nod to the power it carried.

Flowers have never been just decoration. They shift energy.
They remind us what's alive, what's thriving, what's worth tending to.

## My Living Bouquet

There's a walking trail I love. My feet know the rhythm, my mind finds space to breathe.

At the end of the trail, there's a grocery store. I always stop in—grab water, maybe a snack.

And every time, I pass the floral section.

For years, I lingered. Dropped hints to boyfriends. Waiting for someone to just *know* to bring me flowers.

Not for a birthday.
Not for an apology.
Just because.
I wanted that thoughtful, no-occasion kind of romance.

And every time I passed those bouquets, a small voice whispered:
Maybe one day.

Then one day, I stopped waiting.
I wandered into the floral section and ran my fingers along the petals.
I wanted something big. Lush. Overflowing.
But those arrangements were $40 and up—and girl, I was on a budget.
I knew I deserved flowers. But did I really want to blow my whole month's spending plan for one extravagant moment?

So I moved to the value bin.
Smaller bouquets. $5 to $7. They felt light in my hands. A little sad. But I brought one home anyway.

In the vase, it looked sparse—flowers sprawling, swallowed up by empty space. It wasn't enough. The next week, I added another bouquet. Chose colors that complemented the first.

Some flowers had wilted. Others stood in full bloom. I pulled out what had faded. Made room for the new. Let the arrangement shift. And then I did it again. And again.

Over time, my bouquet became a living thing. Never still. Never perfect.

Always changing. Some flowers just opening. Some in full bloom. Some on their way out.

But together?
They were beautiful.

## The Lesson in the Vase

In tending to those flowers, I learned something:
Growth isn't always about starting fresh. Sometimes, it's about knowing what to keep.

For so long, I thought healing meant burning everything down.
Scorching the earth. Starting from nothing.
Unfriend. Block. Delete the pictures. Cut the ties. Start over.
But healing isn't destruction—it's discernment.

Some things still hold value, even if they're no longer what they once were.
Some things are worth honoring before we let them go. Growth isn't about erasure.
It's about learning what to pull, what to preserve, and what still has room to bloom.

Now, I treat my life the way I treat my bouquet. I don't discard everything at the first sign of change. But I don't cling to what's clearly run its course.

I no longer wait for flowers.I choose them. I arrange them. I decide what stays. What goes. What gets the sunlight.

Because I'm not just something to be admired.
I'm something that grows. Endures. Evolves.

Just like them.

# Pussy Don't Fail Me Now

Why do we treat good pussy like a badge of honor, a spell, a safety net?

Why do we believe it's our most powerful form of protection and currency—the card that never declines?

And not just any card.

The Black one.

Even before we cross the threshold into sex, the awareness is there. It hums in the background. *Will it be good? Will I be good?*

That pressure doesn't wait until we're sexually active—it builds over time. Layered by music, jokes, girl talk, and the silence between warnings from the women before us.

I remember going into my first sexual encounter hoping it would be good. Not just for him—but because it felt like it *mattered*.
Like I was auditioning for a role I'd been studying for my whole life.

If it was good, maybe I'd secure my place.
Maybe I'd protect my heart.

Because that's what good pussy felt like back then:

A wild card.
Like pulling a Wild Draw 4 in Uno—you think you've got the upper hand.
You can change the color. Shift the game. Tilt the table.

You believe maybe, just maybe, you've got some control.
Like you can safeguard the love.
Safeguard yourself.

We already had a love full of sparks, false starts, breakups and makeups.
But this time, we hadn't spoken in six months.

That winter, we were both back home.
He emailed me out of the blue—tender, reflective.
Thanking me for everything I'd been to him.
And just like that, we started talking again.

One night, I found myself at his door.
He kissed me the second I walked in and pulled me toward the bedroom.

I didn't enter intimacy until I was twenty-one.
Not because I was scared or ashamed.
But because it *mattered* to me.
I wanted my first time to feel like something.
To hold up to the kind of passion I'd read about in books.

And as we reached the end of our encounter, I remember the moment clearly.
He exhaled, *"This pussy good."*

And something in me shifted.

That was my unofficial initiation into the Good Pussy Club.
It felt like validation.
Like I'd made it.

Like I had joined the ranks of women whose names don't get forgotten.

The ones men think about. Circle back to.
The ones they can't leave alone.

And for a while, I thought that meant power.
Because in that moment, it did.

It felt like access. Like I could ask for anything in that breathless space—and he'd give it. No hesitation.

That's the allure of the Good Pussy Club. It feels like leverage. Like finally, you have a say in the room you've been trying to matter in.

Before that night, I was the good girl. Rule follower. Emotion stuffer.

And he was the cool guy—the one with all the pull. I was still surprised he even liked me back.

But after that night? I was the good girl *with* good pussy.

And that changed everything.

It felt like I finally had some weight in the dynamic. Like I could speak—and be heard.

You know how you trust your GPS in a city you've never driven through? It says turn left, and you just… do it.
No questions asked.

That's what it felt like.
He might've been driving the car, but I had become the navigation system.
Undeniable.

Even the way I spoke to him changed.
My voice dropped into butter—warm, soft, slow.
Each word ribboned around him.

And when he spoke back, I felt like I was unlocking a version of him meant just for me.

His love felt *tangible*.
Reachable.
Touchable.
Holdable.

That night felt like a portal.

But the next time I saw him? I was on the outside.

A few days later, I ran into him at the skating rink.
Skating with *her*.
The girl he told me not to worry about.
You know the one.
The "friend."

And baby, I felt *gutted*.
Like somebody deep fried my heart and didn't pull it back out.

That's when I learned something about the Good Pussy Club:
It has a time limit.

Or more specifically—it has Wi-Fi.

And the connection?
It's strongest when the desire is mutual, the attention locked in, the vibe aligned.

Sometimes it's before sex. Sometimes it's during. Sometimes it lasts a little while after—when the chemicals are still dancing.

But if the sex was the *only* reason they were connecting?
That signal drops. Fast.

One day you're synced—talking daily, sharing secrets, feeling seen.
The next?
You're buffering.

Dry energy. Long replies. Something shifts.

And you realize…
The Wi-Fi was never stable.
You just had a strong connection—for a moment.

That's when it clicked:
I was never in control.
I just had a signal.
And it passed.

But then something else shifted.
The more I grew into myself, the more that power turned inward.

Not tied to how he moaned my name.
Not about performance.
But about *presence*.

About how I felt in my body.
How I came alive.
Not for what it could get me but for how it felt to be *in* me.

Without shame.Without permission.

My voice dropped into something warm and commanding.
   My movements became intentional—like my body had remembered itself.
   That wasn't the Good Pussy Club anymore.
   That was the **Avatar State**.


In *Avatar: The Last Airbender*, the Avatar State is when the character connects to all the power and knowledge of their past selves. It's when they're strongest but also most vulnerable.


If they're harmed in that state, they risk losing everything.


That's what it felt like. I had accessed an alternate version of myself.
Present. Powerful. Embodied.


And I wasn't the first.
Black women have always known this power.
Even when the world refused to name it.


Lucille Bogan knew.
Back in the 1930s, she sang:
*"I got something between my legs'll make a dead man come."*


That wasn't just a lyric.
That was resurrection.
A portal line.


On the surface, about sex.
Underneath? Magic. Myth. Mystery.
The vagina has always been a bridge.
Between life and death. This world and the next.


Lucille wasn't just talking her shit.
She was casting a spell.

Speaking to the divine force Black women have always carried.

And still—the Jezebel myth lingered. We were turned into objects.
Then shamed for how those objects were seen.

So we did what we always do.
We flipped it.
Made it music. Made it comedy. Made it survival. Made it ours.

But even with all that reclaimed power...good pussy still can't save you.

That's why you have to move in the Avatar State *from* your power.
Not chasing.
Not performing.
Not begging to be chosen.
When you open yourself to someone who can't hold that version of you?
You're the one left piecing your spirit back together.

So yeah—good pussy got power.
But the real question isn't *do you feel powerful with it?*
It's: **Can you still feel powerful without it?**

And now that we know how potent it is—how will we use it?

Not as bait.Not as a bargaining chip. Not to beg to be kept.

But as something sacred.
Something you carry.
If it's really that powerful?
Let it walk you through the doors meant for you.
Let it anchor you not just attract them.

Let it remind you of who you are.

Not just what you do to them.
That's the kind of power I want now.
Not just the kind that turns heads.
But the kind that keeps me aligned.
The kind that honors the Avatar State.
The state where I am most alive, most intuitive, most whole.

Because that power was never just about sex.
It was about what happens when I stop shrinking and start channeling.

And the real flex?
Its staying connected to that version of me.
Even after the bodies leave.
Even after the desire fades.
Even after the trance breaks.

That's when I know I'm not just *visiting* the Avatar State.
I've made a *home* there.
Because yeah, good pussy got Wi-Fi.

But the source?
The source doesn't drop signal.
Doesn't get weaker with distance.
Doesn't rely on who's watching or reaching.

The source is steady.
Ancient.
Always on.
And the source… is me.
And *that* never fails.
So yeah—this pussy good. And so are my knees.

# Good Knees Good Knees

My knees have been through a lot.

Hold on... wait a minute. I know that sounds like the start of a joke, but I'm so serious.

These knees? They've dropped it low at parties, buckled in heartbreak, hit the floor in prayer, cracked during squats, and wobbled in joy. They've been scraped, swollen, stretched, and sore. They've held me up when I didn't think I could stand.

And somehow—they're still here.

Still bending. Still bouncing. Still testifying.

My knees remember everything.

Heartache. Praise breaks. Long walks that helped me breathe. Slow dancing with someone I thought I'd love forever. Sprinting toward freedom when I finally left.

These joints aren't just physical—they're spiritual.
They carry story. They carry strength.
I used to move my body because I didn't like it.
I tried to shrink it, fix it, punish it.

Now?
I move because it reminds me I'm still here.
Because motion is not punishment. It's power.
It's not about discipline. It's about devotion.
It reminds me of a power I've felt before—in moments of intimacy, intuition, and embodiment.

But my knees knew it first.
When joy feels far away, my body usually finds it before my mind does.
Before I can talk myself into hope, my hips start swaying to a song I didn't even mean to play.

Before I can process the grief, my feet carry me out for a walk that clears the fog.
Before I can name the breakthrough, my breath deepens during a stretch and something in me exhales for the first time in days.

Joy is smart like that.
She doesn't always knock at the front door. Sometimes she comes in through the body—through rhythm, sway, bounce, breath.

Joy is not passive. It's curated.
We don't dance because we're already happy.
We dance because joy is a practice. A conjuring.
We move to make room for happiness to find us.

Our ancestors didn't wait to feel free before they sang. They moved, they clapped, they shuffled, they stomped—and that movement made freedom real, even if only for a heartbeat.

And we still do it now.

Before colonization, before ships, before trauma rewrote our names—our bodies already knew what to do.

In West African traditions, movement wasn't separate from spirit. Dance was prayer, celebration, mourning, community, initiation. It told stories, honored ancestors, marked transitions, healed pain.The hips and knees led the way—grounded, circular, rooted in the Earth. Our dances weren't designed for performance. They were designed for connection.

When we danced, we weren't just moving—we were communicating. With each other. With the land. With the divine. That knowledge didn't die in the Middle Passage. It migrated. It morphed.

And it lived on—in us.

During slavery, enslaved Africans were forbidden to drum. The slaveholders knew what they were doing. They feared the communication. The rhythm. The power. So they tried to silence it.

But we didn't stop moving. We clapped. We stomped. We slapped our thighs, snapped our fingers, shuffled our feet. We turned our bodies into instruments. This was survival. This was resistance.

The Ring Shout is a perfect example.

A sacred, circular dance where people shuffled counterclockwise, clapping, singing, and calling out to Spirit. No formal instruments—just voice and movement.

The shout wasn't loud in volume, but it was loud in intention. It was praise. Protest. Power. Hidden in plain sight.

And that circular motion? That's not random. That's ancestral. It mirrors African cosmology—life as a cycle, death as a return, time as non-linear.

Even under bondage, we moved in rhythm with the divine.

Tap dancing didn't start as entertainment. It started as survival. When enslaved Africans were brought to the Americas, they carried rhythm with them. Drums were more than music—they were communication. They could signal danger. Send messages across plantations. Even help coordinate escape. White enslavers knew that.

That's why in many places, they banned the drum altogether. They feared what it could do. Feared what we could organize. Feared what we could remember. But rhythm don't die just because an instrument gets taken away.

We became the instrument. We clapped. We stomped. We slapped thighs, patted our chests, shuffled our feet. We used our bodies to keep the beat alive.

Over time, something new was born. African footwork met Irish and Scottish step dances in the tight quarters of bondage—and out of that, tap dancing emerged. Not the flashy Broadway version. The early kind. Raw. Rooted. Real. A new form of expression when words weren't safe. A way to speak when speech could get you killed.

So when people say dance isn't that deep—remind them: We moved when we weren't allowed to talk. We tapped when we weren't allowed to drum. We danced because it was the only way to say, "I'm still here."

Every heel drop carried history.
Every shuffle was a signal.
Every step was a way to stay human when the world tried to strip that away.

This wasn't just art.
It was a coded language.
It was a form of freedom work, hidden in plain sight.

## The World Is Burning and We're Still Line Dancing

Headlines heavy.
Rent high.
Grief thick.
And yet—Black folks are out here putting boots on the ground.
Not marching. Not protesting.
Dancing.

We are at the cookout, the baby shower, the trail ride, the family reunion—stepping in sync like the world ain't falling apart around us. Like joy showed up anyway. Like we decided to be here on purpose.

One-two-step. Rock. Slide. Turn.

Bodies lined up in rhythm. Laughter spilling out. Elbows linked. Feet moving like we still got a reason to. And we do.That's not just fun. That's spiritual muscle memory. It's what happens when survival meets celebration. When collective memory becomes choreography. When grief don't get the final say.

Because joy is not an accident.
Joy is work. Joy is resistance.
Joy is curation.

## Ode to Moving Just Because

And even if there's no divine message in it...
Even if it's not healing old wounds or retelling ancestral stories...
Even if your movement is just silly, small, or sweaty...

Move anyway.
Move for no reason other than the beat felt good.
Move because your knees still bend.
Move because your body asked you to.
Move because stillness started to feel like a cage.

Let joy show up where it wants to—without explanation. Let movement exist without needing to be productive or powerful or poetic.

Let joy just... be.
Because joy for joy's sake?
That's liberation too.


## My Joy Lives in Motion


Sometimes joy looks like me walking three miles and realizing I feel clear again. Sometimes it's dancing in my robe on a slow Sunday morning. Sometimes it's a yoga stretch that opens up more than my hips. Sometimes it's just strutting to a good playlist and remembering I'm that girl—even if my day's been trash.

Movement isn't always about fitness.
Sometimes joy is a squat.
Sometimes it's a sway.
Sometimes it's just remembering my knees still bend.
These knees? They've endured.
They've endured me.

They've bent for love, for grief, for surrender, for survival. They've held weight I had no business carrying. And still—they hold me up. They are my ancestors' wildest dreams in motion. They are the proof that my joy can live inside the same body that once held so much pain.

They are sacred. They are soft. They are strong. Joy, for me, lives in the body first. It starts in the sway of a hip, the bounce of a knee, the breath that comes easier when I move. It's not always loud, and it doesn't always show up right away—but when it does?

It feels like rhythm. Like praise. Like home.
Joy is a muscle. A memory. A practice. A choice.
And when I forget? My knees remember.
They always do.

Life can get heavy, sure.
Bills due—too many at that.
Spirits low. Headlines ugly.
But in spite of it all...

Drop down and get your eagle on, girl.
Like your life is depending on it.
Because it is.

# VII

# Welcome Home

# OFFICIAL GRADUATION AUDIT

### UNIVERSITY OF EMOTIONAL SURVIVAL
### OFFICE OF THE REGISTRAR

**OFFICIAL GRADUATION AUDIT: DOCTORAL CONFERRAL**

**Student Name:** Courtney Shelley
**Student ID:** 0000-FK-NG4
**Program:** Doctor of Reclamation Studies
**Degree Conferral Date:** October 25, 2025
**Dissertation Title:** ~~Eat Yo Own Spaghetti: The Theory & Practice of Fuck Nigga Liberation~~
Eat Yo Own Spaghetti: Reflections on Life, Love and Reclaiming Your Power
**Status:** Cleared for Graduation

**Previously Earned Degrees:**

- **Bachelors in Holding It Down Too Long**
- **Masters of Boundary Reconstruction**

**Comments:**
All program requirements have been fulfilled under extreme emotional duress, chronic gaslighting, and spiritual sabotage.
Candidate demonstrated outstanding resilience, refined intuition, and

231

breakthrough boundary-setting across all enrolled coursework.

Transcript of completed classes appears below.

| Course Code | Course Title | Status | Grade |
|---|---|---|---|
| **FIN 3001** | Financial Betrayal 101: When Your Credit Took the Hit | Completed | A (with trauma) |
| **GAS 4201** | Advanced Gaslighting & Ghosting | Completed | A+ |
| **CHE 4602.00** | Cheating Across Departments: Workplace Edition | Completed (Practicum) | A++ |
| **EMP 3304** | Emotional Withholding & Manipulation | Immersive Residency | A |
| **PSY 4025** | Fuckboy Psychology: Case Study Edition | Completed | A |
| **LAB 4013** | Emotional Labor Without Pay | Completed | A+ |
| **BDR 3107** | Interpersonal Boundary Setting | Retaken 3x | A (Eventually) |
| **TRA 3033** | Applied Clarity & Cognitive Dissonance | Completed | A |

| INT 3900 | Intuitive Intelligence : Ignored Then Honored | Completed | C → A |
|---|---|---|---|
| CRM 4700 | Crisis Management (Jail, Lawyers, Lies) | Completed | A++ |
| HCL 3200 | Healing Without Closure | Completed | A |

| POT 4999 | Abstinence from the Addiction to Potential | In Progress → Completed | A- |
|---|---|---|---|
| SPG 4300 | Spiritual Hygiene & Soul Retrieval | Completed | Honors |
| SFG 8280 | Self Forgiveness | Pass | Current Fellow |
| PAT 3009 | Pattern Recognition: The Helper Complex & The Exploiter | Withdrawn (2016), Incomplete (2019), Pass(2025) | A |

| | | | |
|---|---|---|---|
| **PROJ 4902** | Projection, Deflection, and the Delusional Olympics | Completed | B |
| **CMP 4555** | Triangulation & Comparison as a Manipulation Tactic | Completed | A |
| **PRD 4803** | Public Praise, Private Dismissal: The Psychology of Unequal Treatment | Completed | A |
| **MAM 1864** | Maternal Wounds & the Surrogate Girlfriend Trap | Completed | A |
| **THF 4950** | Intellectual Theft & Accomplishment Appropriation | Survived & Reclaimed | A++ |
| **BABY 4040** | Baby Mama Drama & Paternity Test Avoidance | Capstone Project | A+++ |
| **DNG 4033** | Psychic Damage from Unconfirmed Pregnancies | Independent Study | A |
| **REC 5000** | Reclamation Studies: Thesis Defense | Completed | Honors (Distinction) |

# "Clear Your Lens"

*Valedictorian Speech*
*Delivered by Courtney Shelley, PhD in Reclamation Studies*
*Class of 2025*

Good afternoon to the graduating class of 2025.

To my fellow survivors, self-reclaimers, and lens-clearers—I see you.

We made it.

Now I know... this ain't your typical university.
We didn't have dorm rooms. We had dark nights of the soul.
We didn't pledge sororities. We pledged silence. Then shame. Then finally?
Ourselves.
But today?

Today we walk.
We walk across a stage we built ourselves.
From old journal pages, missed calls, voice memos we never sent, and prayers
we weren't always sure someone was listening to.
When I first enrolled in this program—somewhere around 2013—I didn't
know it had a name.

All I knew was that I loved someone who didn't know how to love me back.

236

And I made that mean something about me.

For years, I kept showing up for a degree because I was told it was a proven method for success... sound familiar.

But each time I thought I was done, another course would restart:

- *Boundary Setting: Retaken 3x.*
- *Pattern Recognition: Withdrawn (2016), Re-enrolled (2023).*
- *Self Forgiveness: Currently a Fellow.*

I didn't pass them all on the first try. But eventually, I did. Technically, I've earned three degrees from this institution:

- A **Bachelor's in Holding It Down Too Long**
- (*emotionally expensive, professionally useless*)
- A **Master's in Boundary Reconstruction**
- (*completed in tears, late-night realizations, and finally saying no*)
- And now? A **Ph.D. in Reclamation Studies**

That bachelor's didn't get me hired anywhere worth being. It got me overworked, underloved, and emotionally bankrupt. But every credit counted—even the ones I didn't want to admit I signed up for.

The biggest shift?
It wasn't just leaving him. It was learning to see it all differently.
**That's what it means to clear your lens.**

Because pain will blur the truth.
Love will photoshop it.
But clarity?
Clarity shows you what was always there.
Not what you *hoped* it was.
Not what you *feared* it might be.

But what it *really* was.

One of the most important classes I took was *Pattern Recognition*.
We had reconnected—this time as "friends."
He started sharing more—claiming transparency as proof of growth.
And he told me about the girl. The one who was in the house during the certified crash-out episode.

Years ago, he had sworn she was just a coworker.
Then, when intimacy was undeniable, he reduced it to "just a fling."
But now? He described how she had lost her mother. How she called him.
How he went with her to the mortuary.

And normally? That's where class would've ended.
Because when you're still enrolled emotionally, you can't see past the haze.
But this time, I had distance. I had clarity.

**My lens was clear.**

So I kept listening.

He said she was a helper. Said she was strong. That she was carrying everything on her own.

And in that moment, it hit me:
She sounded like me.
In fact, she sounded like every woman he'd entangled himself with while I was still on the roster.

We were all the helpers.
The emotional first responders.
The ones holding it down—even while being held down.

238

I used to think he didn't have a type.
The women were all different shapes, aesthetics, vibes.
But he did have a type.
**His type was labor.**

His type was the woman who survived and stayed soft.

And then, something clicked.

It was like finally getting your hands on the syllabus—only to realize you'd been in the wrong class for years.

My beautiful liar didn't just stumble into this dynamic—he *selected* me for it.

Not in spite of who I was, but *because* of it.

And unlike before, when I was seeing through the haze of love or the sting of pain—

This time, my lens was clear.

**Spaghetti Magic?**
That's the elective you take that makes you rethink your whole major.
The one that reminds you: the power was never in the pot—it was in the choosing.
Choosing yourself. Feeding yourself.
Not begging someone to scrape the bottom of their bowl and hand you leftovers.
Choosing to eat your own spaghetti, even if you're the only one at the table.

For a long time, I was just waiting. Waiting for him to finally come home for dinner. Sitting in the kitchen with a full plate in front of me—hot, ready, and made with love. And the only thing stopping me from eating... was me.

239

One day, I realized: I had been starving myself while hoping someone else would get hungry.
And for a while, I was mad that I'd waited so long to finally eat my spaghetti.

But the thing about spaghetti—and we all know this—is that it gets better as it sits.

So I reheated it. Said grace. And ate.
And it was the best damn spaghetti I ever had.
And for anyone waiting for someone to show up to eat, or for anyone trying to forgive themselves for what they allowed when they didn't know better..

It's time to make your plate.

# The To Go Plate

There's an art to fixing the to-go plate.

Anybody who's been to a Black function knows: you don't just fix it—you strategize it.

You clock the layout. You scan the foil pans. You identify who brought what.
You make your main plate, yeah—but you also peep what's going fast.
Because a good to-go plate isn't made at the end of the function.
It's made when the moment is ripe.
Too early? You look greedy.
Too late? You miss out.
It takes discernment.
Because timing matters.

You can't fix your life plate too early—before you've lived enough to know what you even like.

But you also can't wait around thinking everything will still be there.
Love.
Opportunity.
Self.

The moment will pass. And when it does, you need to be ready to pack what you need and take it with you.

241

But the real magic? It's in what you put together.
Some things share space. Others need their own container.
Would you ever put potato salad next to cake?
No. Exactly.
(And if you said yes... seek help.)

Some lessons can touch. Some need boundaries.
You might place forgiveness next to joy.
But betrayal? That might need its own plate so it doesn't leak over everything else.

I used to pack it all—grief, guilt, even what wasn't mine to carry.
But some things don't travel well.
Some things weigh you down more than they feed you.
Some combos surprise you.
Like yams and mac & cheese—sweet and savory, side by side.
That's rage and rest. Two things you didn't think belonged together—but baby, when you let them touch?
That's liberation.

Because that's what this book has really been about.
Learning what to plate together.
What to save for later.
What to throw away.
It's been about timing. Portioning. Balance.
It's been about feeding yourself first.
I spent years fixing everybody else's plate.
Making sure they were full, satisfied, taken care of.
And I was going home hungry.

No more.

This plate right here? This is mine.

And I'm not apologizing for it.
I've earned this meal.
I stayed too long—yes.
I over gave. Over-functioned. Over-performed—yes.
But I also healed. Softened. Screamed. Grew. Danced. Declared.

Some things tasted good in the moment, but I knew deep down—they didn't reheat well.
Just because something hits when it's hot doesn't mean it belongs in your to-go plate.
And now, it's time to pack up what I've learned.

Not because the function is over—but because I want something waiting for me when I get home.

Because I am worth coming home to.
So I'm fixing my to-go plate.

Putting rage and rest together.
Wrapping joy in foil.
Spoonfuls of softness, served next to sharpness.
A slice of forgiveness, topped with boundaries.
Every bite seasoned with self-trust.
And of course, leaving room for my spaghetti.

Because I ain't just eating to survive anymore.
I'm eating to remember.
To restore.
To reclaim.

I gave you my recipe.

That's what this book has been—alchemy, transformation,

a slow simmer of pain into something rich, bold, and worth savoring.

Every ingredient. Every cut. Every slow stir—a step toward reclaiming myself.
I took what tried to break me and made a feast out of it.

But this ain't just about me.
Every woman has her own recipe—her own mix of heartbreak and healing, of lessons learned and love lost, of moments that seared and moments that saved.

So now, I ask you—

**How do you make your spaghetti?**

# Loving My Leftovers

(*Author's Note*)

This book is a collage. A reclamation. A love letter to the younger me.

A love letter to Black women who've had to gather themselves from the floor and still show up shining.

A love letter to Black culture—the rhythm, the language, the survival, the softness we create even in the midst of sorrow.

It's us, in all our complexity. All our power. All our tenderness.

I've always been a writer.

My second-grade teacher, Ms. Binns, saw it in me before I even saw it in myself. She looked past the little Black girl always getting in trouble and saw someone who felt everything deeply. Someone misunderstood by the world, but carrying something important to say.

Instead of punishing me for feeling too much, she did something different.

She gave me a book.

That's where it started. That's where I first learned the power of words—not just in speaking, but in writing, in reading, in imagining. Books became my world. My escape. My way through.

By fifth grade, I was weaving little worlds of my own. My teacher called my writing immersive and encouraged me to submit to competitions—but I never did. Even then, it felt too vulnerable. Like letting people peer into a part of me I wasn't ready to share.

By middle school, I realized something else: writing wasn't just creative.
It was survival.
It was my voice when my real one got tangled.

I've always struggled to express myself in real time—especially when emotions ran high. (If you've read *Ain't Nobody Died*, you already know.) I would bottle things up until they knotted. But writing gave me space to slow down, untangle, and finally say what I needed to say.

In college, I started writing again—but this time, it wasn't fiction.
I was writing the life I longed for.
The love I hadn't experienced yet.
The world I still believed could exist.

Writing was how I held onto hope.
Then came the poetry era—scribbled lines on receipts, order pads, the margins of notebooks. Love and longing I couldn't hold in any longer.

But love changes shape.
I went from writing love notes on napkins to writing dreams I wanted to build with someone. From sweet poems to long letters during deployments, trying to close the distance with words.
And slowly, those words shifted.

I went from love letters to breakup letters.

From soft confessions to five-minute audio messages during arguments—
begging for care, setting boundaries, reaching for safety I never should've
had to beg for.

Eventually, when love fell apart completely, I wrote my way through
heartbreak: journal entries, scribbled paragraphs, voice notes.
Still trying to find my way out of the ache.
Even when I thought I had lost myself, I was still there—writing my way
through.

At one point while writing this book, I found myself back in my childhood
bedroom, rummaging through old drawers.
And that's when I found them:
The remnants.
Old notebooks. Scribbled poems. Crumpled journal entries.
Pieces of a younger me I thought I had buried.

What hit me the hardest?
I didn't even recognize some of it.
The voice was different—but it was still mine.
The girl who dared to dream. Who wrote her feelings out so clearly. Who
never stopped reaching for herself, even when nothing made sense.

In that moment, I felt something unexpected:
Gratitude.
Gratitude for her.
For the girl who kept going.
For the girl who never let go of herself—even when I did.

And now I see it clearly.
Maybe she was right.
In all her scribblings about love. In her poems, her prayers, her quiet
declarations that true love always finds its way home.

She believed it.
And maybe... she wasn't wrong.
I just had to learn that the truest love starts with me.

This book is proof.
Proof that I found my way back to myself.
That I'm still the girl who loves love.
Who feels deeply.
Who writes to understand.

I never lost her—I just had to remember.
And as I type these final words, I feel it deep in my bones:
I got her back.

To my family—thank you. You shaped the way I see the world, the way I love, the way I believe.

To my friends—you held the phone, held space, and held me down. You listened, offered to read my words, reminded me this mattered, and pushed me to keep going.

And to everyone woven into these pages—

The friends who stayed. The ones who left. The folks who picked up the phone. The ones I had to block. The women who walked with me. The ones I imagined holding my hand from the other side.

Yes... even him.

You were part of the story.

And I made it mine.

If this book stirs something in you—if even one sentence, one memory, one moment lights a match inside—
I hope it leads you back to yourself, too.

And when you find you, I hope you never let go.
Because you were never truly lost.
You are already home.

www.ingramcontent.com/pod-product-compliance
Lightning Source LLC
Chambersburg PA
CBHW021717120626
46545CB00004B/1596